The Rampa Story

Lobsang Rampa

The Rampa Story

The present edition is a reproduction of previous publication of this classic work. Minor typographical errors may have been corrected without note, however, for an authentic reading experience the spelling, punctuation, and capitalization have been retained from the original text.

ISBN: 978-1-61895-396-4

Contents

The Incredible Truth

Few books have aroused more controversy in recent years than Lobsang Rampa's THE THIRD EYE, and the other works which have come from his pen.

The reason is simple enough. When an Englishman claims that his body has been taken over by the spirit of a Tibetan Lama, he can reasonably expect mockery. When, in addition, he recounts extraordinary, highly detailed experiences which pre-suppose the possession of personal powers quite outside the laws of nature as we understand them, the reaction not surprisingly becomes an uproar.

But uproars of this kind do sometimes spring from ignorance. To glimpse what was previously unknown is always disturbing. The fact that Dr. Rampa now has many thousands of readers throughout the world is evidence that not all minds are closed against the unfamiliar.

It is for this great body of readers — and, no less, for the skeptics who have been able neither to disprove his story nor to explain how he came by his knowledge if his story is untrue—that Dr. Rampa wrote this, his third book.

THE RAMPA STORY is Lobsang Rampa's reply to all his critics, and every page carries his own unswerving guarantee of the truth.

DEDICATED
to my friends in Howth, Ireland

They were my friends when the "winds blew fair". They were loyal, understanding and greater friends when the unfair winds blew foul, for the people of Ireland know persecution; and they know how to judge Truth. So-

Mr. and Mrs. O'Grady
The Loftus Family
Dr. W. I. Chapman
and
Brud Campbell
(to mention just a few)

THANK YOU!

Author's Foreword

"No bitterness," said Mr. Publisher.

"All right," I thought to myself, "but why should I have any bitterness? I am merely trying to do my job—writing a book as directed."

"Nothing against the Press!" said Mr. Publisher.

"Nothing!!"

"Dear, dear," I said to myself "What does he take me for?" So it shall be. Nothing against the Press. After all, they think they are doing their job, and if they are fed incorrect information, then I suppose they cannot be held wholly responsible. But my idea about the Press? Tut, tut, No. Nothing more about the subject.

This book follows on from The Third Eye, and from Doctor from Lhasa. At the very outset I am going to tell you that this is Truth, not fiction. Everything that I have written in the other two books is true, and is my own personal experience. What I am going to write about concerns the ramifications of the human personality and ego, a matter at which we of the Far East excel.

However, no more Foreword. The book itself is the thing!

Chapter One

The jagged peaks of the hard Himalayas cut deeply into the vivid purple of the Tibetan evening skies. The setting sun, hidden behind that mighty range, threw scintillating, iridescent colors on the long spume of snow perpetually blowing from the highest pinnacles. The air was crystal clear, invigorating, and giving almost limitless visibility.

At first glance, the desolate, frozen countryside was utterly devoid of life. Nothing moved, nothing stirred except the long pennant of snow blowing high above. Seemingly nothing could live in these bleak mountainous wastes. Apparently no life had been here since the beginning of time itself.

Only when one knew, when one had been shown time after time, could one detect—with difficulty the faint trace that humans lived here. Familiarity alone would guide one's footsteps in this harsh, forbidding place. Then only would one see the shadow-enshrouded entrance to a deep and gloomy cave, a cave which was but the vestibule to a myriad of tunnels and chambers honeycombing this austere mountain range.

For long months past, the most trusted of lamas, acting as menial carriers, had painfully trudged the hundreds of miles from Lhasa carrying the ancient Secrets to where they would be forever safe from the vandal Chinese and traitorous Tibetan Communists. Here too, with infinite toil and suffering, had been brought the Golden Figures of past Incarnations to be set up and venerated in the heart of a mountain. Sacred Objects, age-old writings, and the most venerable and learned of priests were here in safety. For years past, with a full knowledge of the coming Chinese invasion, loyal Abbots had periodically met in solemn conclave to test and pick those who should go to the New Home in the far distance. Priest after priest was tested, without his knowledge, and his record examined, so that only the finest and most spiritually advanced should be chosen. Men whose training and faith was such that they could, if need be, withstand the worst tortures that the Chinese could give, without betraying vital information.

So, eventually, from a Communist over-run Lhasa, they had come to their new home. No aircraft carrying war loads would fly this high. No enemy troops could live off this arid land, land devoid of soil, rocky and treacherous with shifting boulders and yawning chasms. Land so high, so poor in oxygen, that only a hardy mountain people could breathe. Here, at last, in the sanctuary of the mountains, was Peace. Peace in which to work to safeguard the future, to preserve the Ancient Knowledge, and to prepare for the time when Tibet should rise again and be free of the aggressor.

Millions of years ago this had been a flame-spewing range of volcanoes erupting rocks and lava over the changing face of the young Earth. The world then was semi plastic and undergoing the birth-pangs of a new age. Over countless years the flames died down and the half molten rocks had cooled. Lava had flowed for the last time, and gaseous jets from the deep interior of the Earth had expelled the remnants into the open air, leaving the endless channels and tunnels bare and empty. A very few had been choked by rock falls, but others had remained intact, glass hard and streaked with traces of once-molten metals. From some walls trickled mountain springs, pure and sparkling in any shaft of light.

For century after century the tunnels and caves had remained bare of life, desolate and lonely, known only to astral-traveling lamas who could visit anywhere and see all. Astral travelers had scoured the country looking for such a refuge. Now, with Terror stalking the land of Tibet, the corridors of old were peopled by the elite of a spiritual people, a people destined to rise again in the fullness of time.

As the first carefully chosen monks wended their way northwards, to prepare a home within the living rock, others at Lhasa were packing the most precious articles, and preparing to leave unobtrusively. From the lamaseries and nunneries came a small trickle of those chosen. In small groups, under cover of darkness, they journeyed to a distant lake, and encamped by its bank to await others.

In the "new home" a New Order had been founded, the School of the Preservation of Knowledge, and the Abbot in charge, a wise old monk of more than a hundred years, had, with ineffable suffering, journeyed to the caves within the mountains. With him had traveled the wisest in the land, the Telepathic Lamas, the Clairvoyants, and the Sages of Great Memory. Slowly, over many months, they had wended their way higher and higher up the mountain ranges, with the air becoming thinner and thinner with the increasing altitude. Sometimes a mile a day was the most their aged bodies could travel, a mile of scrambling over mighty rocks with the eternal wind of the high passes tearing at their robes, threatening to blow them away. Sometimes deep crevices forced a long and arduous detour.

For almost a week the ancient Abbot was forced to remain in a tightly closed yak-hide tent while strange herbs and potions poured out life-saving oxygen to ease his tortured lungs and heart. Then, with superhuman fortitude he continued the appalling journey.

At last they reached their destination, a much reduced band, for many had fallen by the wayside. Gradually they became accustomed to their changed life. The Scribes carefully penned the account of their journey, and the Carvers slowly made the blocks for the hand printing of the books. The Clairvoyants looked into the future, predicting, predicting the future of Tibet and of other countries. These men, of the utmost purity, were in touch with the Cosmos, and the Akashic Record, that Record which tells all of the past and of the immediate present everywhere and all the probabilities for the future. The Telepaths too were busy, sending messages to others in Tibet, keeping in touch telepathically with those of their Order everywhere— keeping in touch with Me!

"Lobsang. Lobsang!" The thought dinned into my head, bringing me back from my reverie. Telepathic messages were nothing to me, they were more common to me than telephone calls, but this was insistent. This was in some way different. Quickly I relaxed, sitting in the Lotus position, making my mind open and my body at ease. Then, receptive to telepathic messages, I waited. For a time there was nothing, just a gentle probing, as if "Someone" were looking through my eyes and seeing. Seeing what? The muddy Detroit River, the tall skyscrapers of Detroit city. The date on the calendar facing me, April 9th, 1960. Again—nothing. Suddenly, as if "Someone" had reached a decision, the Voice came again.

"Lobsang. You have suffered much. You have done well, but there is no time for complacency. There is a task for you yet to do." There was a pause as if the Speaker had been unexpectedly interrupted, and I waited, sick at heart and wholly apprehensive. I had more than enough of misery and suffering during the past years. More than enough of change, of being hunted, persecuted. As I waited I caught fleeting telepathic thoughts from others nearby. The girl tapping her foot impatiently at the bus stop below my window, "Oh, this bus service, it's the worst in the world. Will it never come?" Or the man delivering a parcel at the house next door: "Wonder if I dare ask the Boss for a rise? Millie will sure be mad if I don't get some money for her soon!" Just as I was idly wondering who "Millie" was, much as a person waiting at a telephone thinks idly, the insistent Inner voice came to me again.

"Lobsang! Our decision is made. The hour has come for you to write again. This next book will be a vital task. You must write stressing one theme, that

3

one person can take over the body of another, with the latter person's full consent."

I started in dismay, and almost broke the telepathic contact. Me write again? About that. I was a "controversial figure" and hated every moment as such. I knew that I was all that I claimed to be, that all I had written before was the absolute truth, but how would it help to rake up a story from the lurid Press's silly season? That was beyond me. It left me confused, dazed, and very sick at heart, like a man awaiting execution.

"Lobsang!" The telepathic voice was charged with considerable acerbity now; the rasping asperity was like an electric shock to my bemused brain. "Lobsang! We are in a better position to judge than you; you are enmeshed in the toils of the West. We can stand aside and evaluate. You have but the local news, we have the world."

Humbly I remained silent, awaiting a continuation of the message, agreeing within myself that "They" obviously knew what was right. After some interval, the Voice came again. "You have suffered much unjustly, but it has been in a good cause. Your previous work has brought much good to many, but you are ill and your judgment is at fault and warped on the subject of the next book."

As I listened I reached out for my age-old crystal and held it before me on its dull black cloth. Quickly the glass clouded and became as white as milk. A rift appeared, and the white clouds were parted like the drawing aside of curtains to let in the light of the dawn. I saw as I heard. A distant view of the towering Himalayas, their tops mantled in snow. A sharp sensation of falling so real that I felt my stomach rising within me. The landscape becoming larger, and then, the Cave, the New Home of Knowledge. I saw an Aged Patriarch, a very ancient figure indeed, sitting on a folded rug of yak wool. Although a High Abbot, he was clad simply in a faded, tattered robe, which seemed almost as ancient as he. His high, domed head glistened like old parchment, and the skin of his wrinkled old hands scarce covered the bones which supported it. He was a venerable figure, with a strong aura of power, and with the ineffable serenity which true knowledge gives. Around him, in a circle of which he was the center, sat seven lamas of high degree. They sat in the attitude of meditation, with their palms face-up and their fingers entwined in the immemorial symbolic clasp. Their heads, slightly bowed, all pointed towards me. In my crystal it was as if I were in the same volcanic chamber with them, as if I stood before them. We conversed as though almost in physical contact.

4

"You have aged greatly," said one.

"Your books have brought joy and light to many, do not be discouraged at the few who are jealous and evilly disposed," said another.

"Iron ore may think itself senselessly tortured in the furnace, but when the tempered blade of finest steel looks back it knows better," said a third.

"We are wasting time and energy," said the Aged Patriarch. "His heart is ill within him and he stands in the shadow of the Other World, we must not overtax his strength nor his health for he has his task clear before him."

Again there was a silence. This time it was a healing silence, while the Telepathic Lamas poured life-giving energy into me, energy which I so often lacked since my second attack of coronary thrombosis. The picture before me, a picture of which I seemed to be a part, grew even brighter, almost brighter than reality. Then the Aged Man looked up and spoke. "My Brother," he said, which was an honour indeed, although I too was an Abbot in my own right. "My Brother, we must bring to the knowledge of many the truth that one ego can depart his body voluntarily and permit another ego to take over and reanimate the vacated body. This is your task, to impart this knowledge."

This was a jolt indeed. My task? I had never wanted to give any publicity about such matters, preferring to remain silent even when it would have been to my material advantage to give information. I believed that in the esoterically blind West most people would be better for not knowing of the occult worlds. So many "occult" people that I had met had very little knowledge indeed, and a little knowledge is a dangerous thing. My introspection was interrupted by the Abbot. "As you well know, we are upon the threshold of a New Age, an Age wherein it is intended that Man shall be purified of his dross and shall live at peace with others and with himself. The populations shall be stable, neither rising nor falling and this without warlike intent, for a country with a rising population must resort to warfare in order to obtain more living space. We would have people know how a body may be discarded like an old robe for which the wearer has no further use, and passed on to another who needs such a body for some special purpose."

I started involuntarily. Yes, I knew all about this, but I had not expected to have to write about it. The whole idea frightened me.

The old Abbot smiled briefly as he said: "I see that this idea, this task, finds no favour with you, my Brother. Yet there are recorded many, many instances of 'possession'. That so many such cases are regarded as evil, or black magic is unfortunate and merely reflects the attitude of those who know little about the subject. Your task will be to write so that those who have eyes may read, and those who are ready may know."

"Suicides," I thought. "People will be rushing to commit suicide, either to escape from debt and troubles or to do a favour to others in providing a body."

"No, no, my Brother," said the old Abbot, "You are in error. No one can escape his debt through suicide, and no one can leave his body for another yet, unless there be very special circumstances which warrant it. We must await the full advent of the New Age, and none may rightfully abandon his body until his allotted span has elapsed. As yet, only when Higher Forces permit, may it be done."

I looked at the men before me, watching the play of golden light around their heads, the electric blue of wisdom in their auras, and the interplay of light from their Silver Cords. A picture, in living color, of men of wisdom and of purity. Austere men, ascetic, shut away from the world. Self possessed and self reliant. "All right for them," I mumbled to myself. "They don't have to live through the rough-and-tumble of Western life." Across the muddy Detroit River the roar of traffic came in waves. An early Great Lakes steamer came past my window, the river ice crunching and crackling ahead of it. Western Life? Noise. Clatter. Blaring radios shrieking the alleged merits of one car dealer after another. In the New Home there was peace, peace in which to work, peace in which to think without one having to wonder who — as here — was going to be the next to stab one in the back for a few dollars.

"My Brother," said the Old Man, "We live through the 'rough-and-tumble' of an invaded land wherein to oppose the oppressor is death after slow torture. Our food has to be carried on foot through more than a hundred miles of treacherous mountain paths where a false step or a loose stone could send one tumbling thousands of feet to death. We live on a bowl of tsampa which suffices us for a day. For drink we have the waters of the mountain stream. Tea is a needless luxury which we have learned to do without, for to have pleasures which necessitate risks for others is evil indeed. Look more intently into your crystal, my Brother, and we will endeavor to show you the Lhasa of today."

I arose from my seat by the window, and made sure that the three doors to my room were safely shut. There was no way of silencing the incessant roar

6

of traffic, traffic on this, the riverside of Canada, and the more muted hum of pulsing, bustling Detroit. Between me and the river was the main road, closest to me, and the six tracks of the railroad. Noise? There was no end to it! With one last glance at the scurrying modern scene before me, I closed the Venetian blinds and resumed my seat with my back to the window. The crystal before me was pulsating with blue light, light that changed and swirled as I turned towards it. As I picked it up and touched it briefly to my head to again establish "rapport" it felt warm to my fingers, a sure sign that much energy was being directed to it from an external source.

The face of the Aged Abbot looked benignly upon me and a fleeting smile crossed his face, then, it were as if an explosion occurred. The picture became disoriented, a patchwork of a myriad non-related colors and swirling banners. Suddenly it was as if someone had thrown open a door, a door in the sky, and as if I were standing at that open door. All sensation of "looking in a crystal" vanished. I was there!

Beneath me, glowing softly in the evening sunlight, was my home, my Lhasa. Nestling under the protection of the mighty mountain ranges, with the Happy River running swiftly through the green Valley. I felt again the bitter pangs of homesickness. All the hatreds and hardships of Western Life welled up within me and it seemed that my heart would break. The joys and sorrows and the rigorous training that I had undergone there, the sight of my native land made all my feelings revolt at the cruel lack of understanding of the Westerners.

But I was not there for my own pleasure! Slowly I seemed to be lowered through the sky, lowering as though I were in a gently descending balloon. A few thousand feet above the surface and I exclaimed in horrified amazement. Airfield? There were airfields around the City of Lhasa! Much appeared unfamiliar, and as I looked about me I saw that there were two new roads coming over the mountain ranges, and diminishing in the direction of India. Traffic, wheeled traffic, moved swiftly along. I dropped lower, under the control of those who had brought me here. Lower, and I saw excavations where slaves were digging foundations under the control of armed Chinese. Horror of Horrors! At the very foot of the glorious Potala sprawled an ugly hut-city served by a network of dirt roads. Straggling wires linked the buildings and gave a slovenly, unkempt air to the place. I gazed up at the Potala, and by the Sacred Tooth of Buddha!—the Palace was desecrated by Chinese Communist slogans! With a sob of sick dismay I turned to look elsewhere.

A truck swirled along the road, ran right through me for I was in the astral

7

body, ghostly and insubstantial, and shuddered to a stop a few yards away. Yelling, sloppily dressed Chinese soldiers poured out of the big truck, dragging five monks with them. Loudspeakers on the corners of all the streets began to blare, and at the brazen-voiced commands, the square in which I was standing quickly filled with people. Quickly, because Chinese overseers with whips and bayonets slashed and prodded those who tarried. The crowd, Tibetans and unwilling Chinese colonists, looked dejected and emaciated. They shuffled nervously, and small clouds of dust rose and were borne away on the evening wind.

The five monks, thin and blood-stained, were thrown roughly to their knees. One, with his left eyeball right out of its socket, and dangling on his cheek, was well known to me, he had been an acolyte when I was a lama. The sullen crowd grew silent and still as a Russian-made "jeep" came racing along the road from a building labeled "Department of Tibetan Administration". All was silent and tense as the car circled the crowd and came to a stop about twenty feet behind the truck.

Guards sprang to attention, and an autocratic Chinese stepped arrogantly from the car. A soldier hurried up to him unreeling wire as he walked. Facing the autocratic Chinese, the soldier saluted and held up a microphone. The Governor, or Administrator, or whatever he styled himself, looked disdainfully round before speaking into the instrument. "You have been brought here," he said, "to witness the execution of these five reactionary and subversive monks. No one shall stand in the way of the glorious Chinese people under the able chairmanship of Comrade Mao." He turned away, and the loudspeakers on the top of the truck clicked into silence. The Governor motioned to a soldier with a long, curved sword. He moved to the first prisoner kneeling bound before him. For a moment he stood with his legs apart, testing the edge of his sword with the ball of his thumb. Satisfied, he took his stance, and gently touched the neck of the bound man. Raising the sword high above his head, with the evening sunlight glinting on the bright blade, he brought it down. There was a soggy noise, followed instantly by a sharp 'crack' and the man's head sprang from his shoulders, followed by a bright gout of blood which pulsed, and pulsed again, before dying away to a thin trickle. As the twitching, headless body lay upon the dusty ground, the Governor spat upon it and exclaimed: "So shall die all enemies of the commune!"

The monk with his eyeball dangling upon his cheek raised his head proudly and cried in a loud voice: "Long live Tibet. By the Glory of Buddha it shall rise again."

8

A soldier was about to run him through with his bayonet when the Governor hastily stopped him. With his face contorted with rage, he screamed: "You insult the glorious Chinese people? For that you shall die slowly!" He turned to the soldiers, shouting orders. Men scurried everywhere. Two raced off to a nearby building, and returned, running, with ropes. Other men slashed at the bonds of the tied monk, cutting his arms and legs in the process. The Governor stamped up and down, yelling for more Tibetans to be brought to witness the scene. The loudspeakers blared and blared again, and truckloads of soldiers came bringing men and women and children to "see the justice of the Chinese Comrades". A soldier struck the monk in the face with his gun-butt, bursting the dangling eye and smashing his nose. The Governor, standing idly by, glanced at the other three monks still kneeling bound in the dirt of the road. "Shoot them," he said, "Shoot them through the back of the head and let their bodies lie." A soldier stepped forward and drew his revolver. Placing it just behind a monk's ear he pulled the trigger. The man fell forward, dead, his brains leaking on the ground. Quite unconcerned, the soldier stepped to the second monk and speedily shot him. As he was moving to the third, a young soldier said, "Let me, Comrade, for I have not killed yet." Nodding assent, the executioner stepped aside to allow the young soldier, trembling with eagerness, to take his place. Drawing his revolver, he pointed it at the third monk, shut his eyes, and pulled the trigger. The bullet sped through the man's cheeks and hit a Tibetan spectator in the foot. "Try again," said the former executioner, "and keep your eyes open." By now his hand was trembling so much with fright and shame that he missed completely, as he saw the Governor scornfully watching him. "Put the muzzle of the revolver in his ear, and then shoot," said the Governor. Once again the young soldier stepped to the side of the doomed monk, savagely rammed the muzzle of his gun in his ear and pulled the trigger. The monk fell forward, dead, beside his companions.

The crowd had increased, and as I looked round I saw that the monk whom I knew had been tied by his left arm and left leg to the jeep. His right arm and right leg were tied to the truck. A grinning Chinese soldier entered the jeep and started the engine. Slowly, as slowly as he possibly could, he engaged gear and moved forward. The monk's arm was pulled out straight, rigid as an iron bar, there was a "snick" and it was torn completely from the shoulder. The jeep moved on. With a loud "crack" the hip bone broke, and the man's right leg was torn from his body. The jeep stopped, and the Governor entered. Then it drove off, with the bleeding body of the dying monk bouncing and jolting over the stony road. Soldiers climbed aboard the big truck, and that drove off, trailing behind it a bloody arm and leg.

As I turned away, sickened, I heard a feminine scream from behind a

9

building, followed by a coarse laugh. A Chinese oath as the woman evidently bit her attacker, and a bubbling shriek as she was stabbed in return.

Above me, the dark blue of the night sky, liberally besprinkled with the pinpoints of colored lights which were other worlds. Many of them, as I knew, were inhabited. How many I wondered, were as savage as this Earth? Around me were bodies. Unburied bodies. Bodies preserved in the frigid air of Tibet until the vultures and any wild animals ate them up. No dogs here now to help in that task, for the Chinese had killed them off for food. No cats now guarded the temples of Lhasa, for they too had been killed. Death? Tibetan life was of no more value to the invading Communists than plucking a blade of grass.

The Potala loomed before me. Now, in the faint starlight, the crude slogans of the Chinese blended with the shadows and were not seen. A searchlight, mounted above the Sacred Tombs, glared across the Valley of Lhasa like a malignant eye. The Chakpori, my Medical School, looked gaunt and forlorn. From its summit came snatches of an obscene Chinese song. For some time I remained in deep contemplation. Unexpectedly, a Voice said: "My Brother, you must come away now, for you have been absent long.

As you rise, look about you well."

Slowly I rose into the air, like thistledown bobbing in a vagrant breeze. The moon had risen now, flooding the Valley and mountain peaks with pure and silvery light. I looked in horror at ancient lamaseries, bombed and untenanted, with all the debris of Man's earthly possessions strewn about uncared for. The unburied dead lay in grotesque heaps, preserved by the eternal cold. Some clutched prayer wheels, some were stripped of clothing and ripped into tattered shreds of bloody flesh by bomb blast and metal splinters. I saw a Sacred Figure, intact, gazing down as if in compassion at the murderous folly of mankind.

Upon the craggy slopes, where the hermitages clung to the sides of the mountains in loving embrace, I saw hermitage after hermitage which had been despoiled by the invaders. The hermits, immured for years in solitary darkness in search of spiritual advancement, had been blinded on the instant when sunlight had entered their cells. Almost without exception, the hermit was stretched dead beside his ruined home, with his life-long friend and servant stretched dead beside him.

I could look no more. Carnage? Senseless murder of the innocent, defenseless monks? What was the use? I turned away and called upon those who guided me to remove me from this graveyard.

10

My task in life, I had known from the start, was in connection with the human aura, that radiation which entirely surrounds the human body, and by its fluctuating color shows the Adept if a person is honorable or otherwise. The sick person could have his or her illness seen by the colors of the aura. Everyone must have noticed the haze around a street light on a misty night. Some may even have noticed the well-known "corona discharge" from high tension cables at certain times. The human aura is somewhat similar. It shows the life force within. Artists of old painted a halo, or nimbus round the head of saints. Why? Because they could see the aura of those people. Since the publication of my first two books people have written to me from all over the world, and some of those people can also see the aura.

Years ago a Dr. Kilner, researching at a London Hospital, found that he could, under certain circumstances, see the aura. He wrote a book about it. Medical science was not ready for such a discovery, and all that he had discovered was hushed up. I too, in my way, am doing research, and I visualize an instrument which will enable any medical man or scientist to see the aura of another and cure "incurable" illnesses by ultra-sonic vibrations. Money, money, that is the problem. Research always was expensive!

And now, I mused, they want me to take on another task! About a change of bodies!

Outside my window there was a shuddering crash which literally shook the house. "Oh," I thought, "The railroad men are shunting again. There will be no more quiet for a long time." On the river a Great Lakes freight steamer hooted mournfully-like a cow mooing for her calf-and from the distance came the echoing response of another ship.

"My Brother!" The Voice came to me again, and hastily I gave my attention to the crystal. The old men were still sitting in a circle with the Aged Patriarch in the center. Now they were looking tired, exhausted would perhaps describe their condition more accurately, for they had transmitted much power in order to make this impromptu, unprepared trip possible.

"My Brother, you have seen clearly the condition of our country. You have seen the hard hand of the oppressor. Your task, your two tasks are clear before you and you can succeed at both, to the glory of our Order."

The tired old man was looking anxious. He knew — as I knew — that I could with honor refuse this task. I had been greatly misunderstood through the lying tales spread by an ill-disposed group. Yet I was very highly clairvoyant, very highly telepathic. Astral traveling to me was easier than walking. Write? Well, yes, people could read what I wrote and if they could not all believe, then those who were sufficiently evolved would believe and know the truth.

"My Brother," said the Old Man, softly, "Even though the unevolved, the unenlightened, pretend to believe that you write fiction, enough of the Truth will get to their sub-conscious and—who knows?—the small seed of truth may blossom in this or in their next life. As the Lord Buddha Himself has said in the Parable of the Three Chariots, the end justifies the means."

The Parable of the Three Chariots! What vivid memories that brought back to me. How clearly I remember my beloved guide and friend, the Lama Mingyar Dondup instructing me at the Chapkori.

An old medical monk had been easing the fears of a very sick woman with some harmless "white lie". I, young and inexperienced, had, with smug complacency, been expressing shocked surprise that a monk should tell an untruth even in such an emergency. My Guide had come along to me, saying, "Let us go to my room, Lobsang. We can with profit turn to the Scriptures." He smiled at me with his warm, benevolent aura of contentment as he turned and walked beside me to his room far up, overlooking the Potala.

"Tea and Indian cakes, yes, we must have refreshment, Lobsang, for with refreshment you can also digest information." The monk-servant, who had seen us enter, appeared unbidden with the delicacies which I liked and which I could only obtain through the good offices of my Guide.

For a time we sat and talked idly, or rather I talked as I ate. Then, as I finished, the illustrious Lama said: "There are exceptions to every rule, Lobsang, and every coin or token has two sides. The Buddha talked at length to His friends and disciples, and much that He said was written down and preserved. There is a tale very applicable to the present. I will tell it to you." He resettled himself, cleared his throat, and continued:

"This is the tale of the Three Chariots. Called so because chariots were greatly in demand among the boys of those days, just as stilts and Indian sweet cakes are now. The Buddha was talking to one of His followers named Sariputra. They were sitting in the shade of one of the large Indian trees discussing truth and untruth, and how the merits of the former are sometimes outweighed by the kindness of the latter.

"The Buddha said, 'Now, Sariputra, let us take the case of a very rich man, a man so rich that he could afford to gratify every whim of his family. He is an

12

old man with a large house and with many sons. Since the birth of those sons he has done everything to protect them from danger. They know not danger and they have not experienced pain. The man left his estate and his house and went to a neighboring village on a matter of business. As he returned he saw smoke rolling up into the sky. He hurried faster and as he approached his home he found that it was on fire. All the four walls were on fire, and the roof was burning. Inside the house his sons were still playing, for they did not understand the danger. They could have got out but they did not know the meaning of pain because they had been so shielded; they did not understand the danger of fire because the only fire they had seen had been in the kitchens.

" 'The man was greatly worried for how could he alone get into the house and save his sons? Had he entered, he could perhaps have carried out one only, the others would have played and thought it all a game. Some of them were very young, they might have rambled and walked into the flames they had not learned to fear. The father went to the door and called to them, saying, "Boys, boys, come out. Come here immediately."

" 'But the boys did not want to obey their father, they wanted to play, they wanted to huddle in the center of the house away from the increasing heat which they did not understand. The father thought: "I know my sons well, I know them exactly, the differences in their characters, their every shade of temperament; I know they will only come out if they think there is some gain, some new toy here." And so he went back to the door and called loudly: "Boys, boys, come out, come out immediately. I have toys for you here beside the door. Bullock chariots, goat chariots, and a chariot as fleet as the wind because it is drawn by a deer. Come quickly or you shall not have them."

" 'The boys, not fearing the fire, not fearing the dangers of the flaming roof and walls, but fearing only to lose the toys, came rushing out. They came rushing, scrambling, pushing each other in their eagerness to be first to reach the toys and have first choice. And as the last one left the building, the flaming roof fell in amid a shower of sparks and debris.

"The boys heeded not the dangers just surmounted, but set up a great clamor. "Father, father, where are the toys which you promised us? Where are the three chariots! We hurried and they are not here. You promised, father."

"The father, a rich man to whom the loss of his house was no great blow, now that his sons were safe, hurried them off and bought them their toys, the chariots, knowing that his artifice had saved the lives of his sons.'

13

"The Buddha turned to Sariputra and said, 'Now Sariputra, was not that artifice justified? Did not that man by using innocent means, justify the end? Without his knowledge his sons would have been consumed in the flames:

"Sariputra turned to the Buddha and said, 'Yes, Oh Master, the end well justified the means and brought much good.' "

The Lama Mingyar Dondup smiled at me as he said, "You were left for three days outside the Chakpori, you thought you were barred from entry, yet we were using a test on you, a means which was justified in the end, for you progress well."

I too am using "a means which will be justified in the end". I am writing this, my true story — The Third Eye and Doctor from Lhasa are absolutely true also — in order that I may later continue with my aura work. So many people have written to ask why I write that I give them the explanation; I write the truth in order that Western people may know that the Soul of man is greater than these sputniks, or fizzling rockets. Eventually Man will go to other planets by astral travel as I have done! But Western Man will not so go while all he thinks of is self gain, self advancement and never mind the rights of the other fellow. I write the truth in order that I may later advance the cause of the human aura. Think of this (it will come), a patient walks into a doctor's consulting room. The doctor does not bother to make any enquiries, he just takes out a special camera and photographs the aura of the patient. Within a minute or so, this non-clairvoyant medical practitioner has in his hand a color-photograph of his patient's aura. He studies it, its striations and shades of color, just as a psychiatrist studies the recorded brain waves of a mentally sick person.

The general practitioner, having compared the color-photograph with standard charts, writes down a course of ultra-sonic and color spectrum treatments which will repair the deficiencies of the patient's aura. Cancer? It will be cured. T.B.? That too will be cured. Ridiculous? Well, just a short time ago it was "ridiculous" to think of sending radio waves across the Atlantic. "Ridiculous" to think of flying at more than a hundred miles an hour. The human body would not stand the strain, they said. "Ridiculous" to think of going into space. Monkeys have already. This "ridiculous" idea of mine. I have seen it working!

The noises from without penetrated my room, bringing me back to the present. Noises? Shunting trains, a screaming fire engine whizzed by, and loud-talking people hasten in to the bright lights of a local place of entertainment. "Later," I tell myself, "when this terrible clamor stops, I will use the crystal and will tell Them that I will do as they ask."

14

A growing "warm-feeling" inside tells me that "They" already know, and are glad.

So, here as it is directed, the truth, The Rampa Story.

Chapter Two

TIBET, at the turn of the century, was beset by many problems. Britain was making a great uproar, shouting to all the world that Tibet was too friendly with Russia, to the detriment of British Imperialism. The Czar of all the Russia's was shrieking in the vast halls of his palace in Moscow, complaining vociferously that Tibet was becoming too friendly with Britain. The Royal Court of China resounded with fevered accusations that Tibet was being too friendly with Britain and with Russia and was most certainly not friendly enough with China.

Lhasa swarmed with spies of various nations, poorly disguised as mendicant monks or pilgrims, or missionaries, or anything which seemed to offer a plausible excuse for being in Tibet at all. Sundry gentlemen of assorted races met deviously under the dubious cover of darkness to see how they could profit by the troubled international situation. The Great Thirteenth, the Thirteenth Dalai Lama Incarnation and a great statesman in His own right, kept his temper and the peace and steered Tibet clear of embroilment. Polite messages of undying friendship, and insincere offers of "protection" cross the Sacred Himalayas from the heads of the leading nations of the world.

Into such an atmosphere of trouble and unrest I was born. As Grandmother Rampa so truly said, I was born to trouble and have been in trouble ever since, and hardly any of it of my own making! The Seers and Sooth-Sayers were loud in their praise of "the boy's" inborn gifts of clairvoyance and telepathy. "An exalted ego," said one. "Destined to leave his name in history," said another. "A Great Light to our Cause," said a third. And I, at that early age, raised up my voice in hearty protest at being so foolish as to be born once again. Relatives, as soon as I was able to understand their speech, took every opportunity to remind me of the noise I made; they told me with glee that mine was the most raucous, the most unmusical musical voice that it had been their misfortune to hear.

Father was one of the leading men of Tibet. A nobleman of high degree, he had considerable influence in the affairs of our country. Mother, too, through her side of the family exercised much authority in matters of policy. Now, looking back over the years, I am inclined to think that they were almost as important as Mother thought, and that was of no mean order.

My early days were spent at our home near the Potala, just across the Kaling

Chu, or Happy River. "Happy" because it gave life to Lhasa as it ran chuckling over many brooks, and meandered in rivulet form through the city. Our home was well wooded, well staffed with servants, and my parents lived in princely splendor. I—well I was subjected to much discipline, much hardship. Father had become greatly soured during the Chinese invasion in the first decade of the century, and he appeared to have taken an irrational dislike to me. Mother, like so many society women throughout the world, had no time for children, looking upon them as things to be got rid of as speedily as possible, and then parked on some hired attendant.

Brother Paljor did not stay with us long; before his seventh birthday he left for "The Heavenly Fields" and Peace. I was four years of age then, and Father's dislike for me seemed to increase from that time. Sister Yasodhara was six at the time of the passing of our brother, and we both bemoaned, not the loss of our brother, but the increased discipline which started at his passing.

Now my family are all dead, killed by the Chinese Communists My sister was killed for resisting the advances of the invaders. My parents for being landowners. The home from whence I gazed wide-eyed over the beautiful parkland has been made into dormitories for slave workers. In one wing of the house are women workers, and in the right wing are men. All are married, and if husband and wife behave and do their quota of work, they can see each other once a week for half an hour, after which they are medically examined.

But in the far-off days of my childhood these things were in the future, something which was known would happen but which, like death at the end of one's life, did not obtrude too much. The Astrologers had indeed foretold these happenings, but we went about our daily life blissfully oblivious of the future.

Just before I was seven years of age, at the age when my brother left this life, there was a huge ceremonial party at which the State Astrologers consulted their charts and determined what my future was going to be. Everyone who was "anything" was there. Many came uninvited by bribing servants to let them in. The crush was so thick that there was hardly room to move in our ample grounds.

The priest fumbled and bumbled, as priests will, and put on an impressive show before announcing the outstanding points of my career. In fairness I must state that they were absolutely right in everything unfortunate which they said. Then they told my parents that I must enter the Chakpori Lamasery to be trained as a Medical Monk.

My gloom was quite intense, because I had a feeling that it would lead to trouble. No one listened to me, though, and I was shortly undergoing the ordeal of sitting outside the Lamasery gate for three days and nights just to see if I had the endurance necessary to become a medical monk. That I passed the test was more a tribute to my fear of Father than of my physical stamina. Entry to the Chakpori was the easiest stage. Our days were long, it was hard indeed to have a day which started at midnight, and which required us to attend services at intervals throughout the night as well as throughout the day. We were taught the ordinary academic stuff, our religious duties, matters of the metaphysical world, and medical lore, for we were to become medical monks. Our Eastern cures were such that Western medical thought still cannot understand them. Yet—Western pharmaceutical firms are trying hard to synthesize the potent ingredients which are in the herbs we used. Then, the age-old Eastern remedy, now artificially produced in a laboratory, will have a high-sounding name and will be hailed as an example of Western achievement.

Such is progress.

When I was eight years of age I had an operation which opened my "Third Eye", that special organ of clairvoyance which is moribund in most people because they deny its existence. With this "eye" seeing, I was able to distinguish the human aura and so divine the intention of those around me. It was—and is!—most entertaining to listen to the empty words of those who pretended friendship for self gain, yet truly had black murder in their hearts. The aura can tell the whole medical history of a person. By determining what is missing from the aura, and replacing the deficiencies by special radiations, people can be cured of illness.

Because I had stronger than usual powers of clairvoyance I was very frequently called upon by the Inmost One, the Great Thirteenth Incarnation of the Dalai Lama, to look at the aura of those who visited Him "in friendship". My beloved Guide, the Lama Mingyar Dondup, a very capable clairvoyant, trained me well. He also taught me the greatest secrets of astral traveling, which now to me is easier than walking. Almost anyone, no matter what they call their religion, believes in the existence of a "soul" or "other body". Actually there are several "bodies" or "sheaths", but the exact number does not concern us here. We believe —rather, we know! that-it is possible to lay aside the ordinary physical body (the one that supports the clothes!) and travel anywhere, even beyond the Earth, in the astral form.

Everyone does astral traveling, even the ones who think it is "all nonsense"! It is as natural as breathing. Most people do it when they are asleep and so,

18

unless they are trained, they know nothing about it. How many people, in the morning, exclaim: "Oh! I had such a wonderful dream last night, I seemed to be with So-and-so. We were very happy together and she said she was writing. Of course it is all very vague now!" And then, usually in a very few days a letter does arrive. The explanation is that one of the persons traveled astrally to the other, and because they were not trained, it became a "dream". Almost anyone can astral travel. How many authenticated cases there are of dying persons visiting a loved one in a dream in order to say good-bye. Again, it is astral traveling. The dying person, with the bonds of the world loosened, easily visits a friend in passing.

The trained person can lie down and relax and then ease off the ties that chain the ego, or companion body, or soul, call it what you will, it is the same thing. Then, when the only connection between is the "Silver Cord", the second body can drift off, like a captive balloon at the end of its line. Wherever you can think of, there you can go, fully conscious, fully alert, when you are trained. The dream state is when a person astral travels without knowing it, and brings back a confused, jumbled impression. Unless one is trained, there are a multitude of impressions con- stantly being received by the "Silver Cord" which confuses the "dreamer" more and more. In the astral you can go anywhere, even beyond the confines of the Earth, for the astral body does not breathe, nor does it eat. All its wants are supplied by the "Silver Cord" which, during life, constantly connects it to the physical body.

The "Silver Cord" is mentioned in the Christian Bible: "Lest the 'Silver Cord' be severed, and the 'Golden Bowl' be shattered." The "Golden Bowl" is the halo or nimbus around the head of a spiritually evolved person. Those not spiritually evolved have a halo of a very different color! Artists of old painted a golden halo around the pictures of saints because the artists actually saw the halo, otherwise he would not have painted it. The halo is merely a very small part of the human aura, but is more easily seen because it is usually much brighter.

If scientists would investigate astral travel and auras, instead of meddling with fizzling rockets which so often fail to go into orbit, they would have the complete key to space travel. By astral projection they could visit another world and so determine the type of ship needed to make the journey in the physical, for astral travel has one great drawback; one cannot take any material object nor can one return with any material object. One can only bring back knowledge. So—the scientists will need a ship in order to bring back live specimens and photographs with which to convince an incredulous world, for people cannot believe a thing exists unless they can tear it to pieces in order to prove that it might be possible after all.

19

I am particularly reminded of a journey into space which I took. This is absolutely true, and those who are evolved will know it as such. It does not matter about the others, they will learn when they reach a greater stage of spiritual maturity.

This is an experience which happened some years ago when I was in Tibet studying at the Chakpori Lamasery. Although it happened many years ago, the memory of it is as fresh in my mind as if it happened but yesterday.

My Guide, the Lama Mingyar Dondup, and a fellow lama, actually a close friend of mine named Jigme, and I, were upon the roof of the Chakpori, on Iron Mountain, in Lhasa, Tibet. It was a cold night indeed, some forty degrees below zero. As we stood upon the exposed roof the shrieking wind pressed our robes tightly against our shivering bodies. At the side of us away from the wind our robes streamed out like Prayer Flags, leaving us chilled to the marrow, threatening to pull us over the precipitous mountainside.

As we looked about us, leaning heavily against the wind to maintain our balance, we saw the dim lights of Lhasa city in the distance, while off to our right the lights of the Potala added to the mystical air of the scene. All the windows seemed to be adorned with gleaming butter lamps, which even though protected by the mighty walls, wavered and danced at the bidding of the wind. In the faint star- light the golden roofs of the Potala were reflecting and glinting as if the Moon itself had descended and played among the pinnacles and tombs atop the glorious building.

But we shivered in the bitter cold, shivered, and wished that we were warm in the incense-laden air of the temple beneath us. We were on the roof for a special purpose, as the Lama Mingyar Dondup enigmatically put it. Now he stood between us, seemingly as firm as the mountain itself, as he pointed upwards at a far distant star—a red looking world—and said, "My brothers this is the star Zhoro, an old, old planet, one of the oldest in this particular system. Now it is approaching the end of its long lifetime".

He turned to us with his back to the biting wind, and said, "You have studied much in astral traveling. Now, together, we will travel in the astral to that planet. We will leave our bodies here upon this windswept roof, and we will move up beyond the atmosphere, beyond even Time."

So saying he led the way across the roof to where there was some slight shelter afforded by a projecting cupola of the roof. He lay down and bade us to lie beside him. We wrapped our robes tightly around us and each held the hand of the other. Above us was the deep purple vault of the Heavens, speckled with faint pin-pricks of light, colored light, because all planets have different lights when seen in the clear night air of Tibet. Around us was the shrieking wind, but our training had always been severe, and we thought naught of remaining on that roof. We knew that this was not to be an ordinary journey into the astral, for we did not often leave our bodies thus exposed to inclement weather. When a body is uncomfortable the ego can travel further and faster and remember in greater detail. Only for small transworld journeys does one relax and make the body comfortable.

My Guide said, "Now let us clasp our hands together, and let us project ourselves together beyond this Earth. Keep with me and we will journey far and have unusual experiences this night."

We lay back and breathed in the accepted pattern for astral traveling release. I was conscious of the wind screaming through the cords of the Prayer Flags which fluttered madly above us. Then, all of a sudden, there was a jerk, and I felt no more the biting fingers of the chill wind. I found myself floating as if in a different time, above my body, and all was peaceful. The Lama Mingyar Dondup was already standing erect in his astral form, and then, as I looked down, I saw my friend Jigme also leaving his body. He and I stood and made a link to join us to our guide the Lama Mingyar Dondup. This link, called ectoplasm is manufactured from the astral body by thought. It is the material from which mediums produce spirit manifestations.

The bond completed, we soared upwards, up into the night sky; I, ever inquisitive, looked down. Beneath us, streaming beneath us, were our Silver Cords, those endless cords which join the physical and the astral bodies during life. We flew on and on, upwards. The Earth receded. We could see the corona of the sun peering across the far ridge of the Earth in what must have been the Western world, the Western world into which we had so extensively traveled in the astral. Higher we went and then we could see the outlines of the oceans and continents in the sunlit part of the world. From our height the world now looked like a crescent moon, but with the Aurora Borealis, or Northern Lights, flashing across the poles.

We moved on and on, faster and faster, until we out- stripped the speed of light for we were disembodied spirits, soaring ever onwards, approaching almost the speed of thought. As I looked ahead of me I saw a planet, huge and menacing and red, straight in front of me. We were falling towards it at a speed impossible to calculate. Although I had had much experience of astral traveling I felt pangs of alarm. The astral form of the Lama Mingyar Dondup chuckled telepathically and said, "Oh Lobsang, if we were to hit that planet it would not hurt them or us. We should go straight through it, there would be no bar."

At last we found ourselves floating above a red, desolate world; red rocks, red sand in a tideless red sea. As we sank down towards the surface of this world we saw strange creatures like huge crabs moving lethargically along the water's edge. We stood upon that red rock shore and looked upon the water, tideless, deadly, with red scum upon it, stinking scum. As we watched, the turbid surface rippled unwillingly, and rippled again, and a strange unearthly creature emerged, a creature also red, heavily armored, and with remarkable joints. It groaned as if tired and dispirited, and reaching the red sand, it flopped down by the side of the tideless sea. Above our heads a red sun glowed dully casting fearful, blood-red shadows, harsh and garish. About us there was no movement, no sign of life other than the strange shelled creatures which lay half-dead on the ground. Even though I was in the astral body I shivered in apprehension as I gazed about me. A red sea upon which floated red scum, red rocks, red dying embers of a fire, a fire which was about to flicker into nothingness.

The Lama Mingyar Dondup said, "This is a dying world. There is no longer rotation here. This world floats derelict in the sea of Space, a satellite to a dying sun, which is soon to collapse, and thus to become a dwarf star without life, without light, a dwarf star which eventually will collide with another star, and from those another world shall be born. I have brought you here because yet in this world there is life of a high order, a life which is here for research and investigation of phenomena of this sort. Look about you."

He turned and pointed with his right hand to the far distance, and we saw three immense towers reaching up into the red, red sky, and on the very top of those towers three gleaming crystal balls glowed and pulsated with clear, yellow light, as if they were alive.

As we stood there wondering one of the lights changed, one of the spheres turned a vivid electric blue. The Lama Mingyar Dondup said, "Come, they are bidding us welcome. Let us descend into the ground to where they are living in an underground chamber."

Together we moved toward the base of that tower, and then, as we stood beneath the framework we saw there was an entrance heavily secured with some strange metal which glimmered and stood out like a scar upon that red and barren land. We moved through it, for metal, or rocks, or anything is no bar to those in the astral. We moved through and traversed long red corridors of dead rock until at last we stood in a very large hall, a hall surrounded by charts and maps, and strange machines and instruments. In the center there was a long table at which sat nine very aged men, all unlike each other. One was tall and thin, and with a pointed head, a conical head. Yet another was

22

short and very solid looking. Each of these men was different. It was clear to us that each man was of a different planet, of a different race. Human? Well perhaps humanoid would be a better word with which to describe them. They were all human, but some were more human than others.

We became aware that all nine were looking fixedly in our direction. "Ah," said one telepathically, "we have visitors from afar. We saw you land upon this, our research station, and we bid you welcome."

"Respected Fathers," said the Lama Mingyar Dondup, "I have brought to you two who have just entered upon the state of Lamahood and who are earnest students in search of knowledge."

"They are indeed welcome," said the tall man, who was apparently the leader of the group. "We will do anything to help as we have helped you with others previously."

This was indeed news to me because I had no idea that my Guide did such extensive astral traveling through celestial places.

The shorter man was looking at me, and smiled. He said in the universal language of telepathy, "I see, young man, that you are greatly intrigued by the difference in our appearances."

"Respected Father," I replied, somewhat overawed by the ease with which he had divined my thoughts, thoughts which I had tried hard to conceal. "That is indeed a fact. I marvel at the disparity of sizes and shapes between you, and it occurred to me that you could not all be men of Earth."

"You have perceived correctly," said the short man. "We are all human, but due to environment we have altered our shapes and our stature somewhat, but can you not see the same thing on your own planet, where upon the land of Tibet there are some monks whom you employ as guards who are seven feet tall. Yet upon another country of that world, you have people who are but half that stature, and you call them pygmies. They are both human; they are both able to reproduce each with the other, notwithstanding any difference in size, for we are all humans of carbon molecules. Here in this particular Universe everything depends upon the basic molecules of carbon and hydrogen for these two are the bricks composing the structure of your Universe. We who have traveled in other Universes far beyond this particular branch of our nebulae know that other Universes use different bricks. Some use silicon, some use gypsum, some use other things, but they are different from people of this Universe, and we find to our sorrow that our thoughts are not always in affinity with them."

The Lama Mingyar Dondup said, "I have brought these two young lamas here so that they can see the stages of death and decay in a planet which has exhausted its atmosphere, and in which the oxygen of that atmosphere has combined with metals to burn them and to reduce everything thing to an impalpable dust."

"That is so," said the tall man. "We would like to point out to these young men that every thing that is born must die. Everything lives for its allotted span, and that allotted span is a number of units of life. A unit of life in any living creature is a heartbeat of that creature. The life of a planet is 2,700,000,000 heartbeats, after which the planet dies, but from the death of a planet others are born. A human, too, lives for 2,700,000,000 heartbeats, and so does the lowliest insect. An insect which lives for but twenty-four hours has, during that time, had 2,700,000,000 heartbeats. A planet— they vary, of course—but one planet may have one heartbeat in 27,000 years, and after that there will be a convulsion upon that world as it shakes itself ready for the next heartbeat. All life, then," he went on, "has the same span, but some creatures live at rates different from those of others. Creatures upon Earth, the elephant, the tortoise, the ant and the dog, they all live for the same number of heartbeats, but all have hearts beating at different speeds, and thus they may appear to live longer or to live less."

Jigme and I found this extremely enthralling, and it explained so much to us that we had perceived upon our native land of Tibet. We had heard in the Potala about the tortoise which lives for so many years, and about the insect which lived for but a summer's evening. Now we could see that their perceptions must have been speeded up to keep pace with their speeding hearts.

The short man who seemed to look upon us with considerable approval, said, "Yes, not only that, but many animals represent different functions of the body. The cow, for instance, as anyone can see, is merely a walking mammary gland, the giraffe is a neck, a dog—well, anyone knows what a dog is always thinking of—sniffing the wind for news as his sight is so poor—and so a dog can be regarded as a nose. Other animals have similar affinities to different parts of one's anatomy. The ant-eater of South America could be looked upon as a tongue."

For some time we talked telepathically, learning many strange things, learning with the speed of thought as one does in the astral. Then at last the Lama Mingyar Dondup stood up and said it was time to leave.

Beneath us as we returned the golden roofs of the Potala gleamed in the

24

frosty sunlight. Our bodies were stiff, heavy and difficult to work with their half frozen joints. "And so," we thought, as we stumbled to our feet, "another experience, another journey has ended. What next?"

A science at which we Tibetans excelled was healing by herbs. Always, until now, Tibet has been shut off from foreigners, and our fauna and flora have never been explored by the foreigners. On the high plateaus grow strange plants. Curare, and the "recently discovered" mescalin, for instance, were known in Tibet centuries ago. We could cure many of the afflictions of the Western world, but first the people of the Western world would have to have a little more faith. But most of the Westerners are mad anyway, so why bother?

Every year parties of us, those who had done best at their studies went on herb-gathering expeditions. Plants and pollens, roots and seeds, were carefully gathered, treated, and stored in yak-hide sacks. I loved the work and studied well. Now I find that the herbs I knew so well cannot be obtained here.

Eventually I was considered fit to take the Ceremony of the Little Death, which I wrote about in The Third Eye. By special rituals I was placed in a state of cataleptic death, far beneath the Potala, and I journeyed into the past, along the Akashic Record. I journeyed, too, to the lands of the Earth. But let me write it as it felt to me then.

The corridor in the living rock hundreds of feet beneath the frozen earth was dank, dank and dark with the darkness of the tomb itself. I moved along its length drifting like smoke in the blackness, and with increasing familiarity with that blackness I perceived at first indistinctly the greenish phosphorescence of moldering vegetation clinging to the rock walls. Occasionally where the vegetation was most prolific and the light the brightest I could catch a yellow gleam from the gold vein running the length of this rocky tunnel.

I drifted along soundlessly without consciousness of time, without thought of anything except that I must go farther and farther into the interior of the earth, for this was a day which was momentous to me, a day when I was returning from three days in the astral state. Time passed and I found myself deeper, deeper in the subterranean chamber in increasing blackness, a blackness which seemed to sound, a blackness which seemed to vibrate.

In my imagination I could picture the world above me, the world to which I was now returning. I could visualize the familiar scene now hidden by total darkness. I waited, poised in the air like a cloud of incense smoke in a temple. Gradually, so gradually, so slowly that it was some time before I could even perceive it, a sound came down the corridor, the vaguest of sounds, but gradually swelling and increasing in intensity. The sound of chanting, the sound of silver bells, and the muffled "shush-shush" of leather- bound feet. At last, at long last, an eerie wavering light appeared glistening along the walls of the tunnel. The sound was becoming louder now. I waited poised above a rock slab in the darkness. I waited.

Gradually, oh so gradually, so painfully slowly, moving figures crept cautiously down the tunnel towards me. As they came closer I saw that they were yellow-robed monks bearing aloft glaring torches, precious torches from the temple above with rare resin woods and incense sticks bound together giving a fragrant scent to drive away the odors of death and of decay, bright lights to dim and make invisible the evil glow of the rank vegetation.

Slowly the priests entered the underground chamber. Two moved to each of the walls near the entrance and fumbled on the rocky ledges. Then one after the other flickering butter lamps sprang into life. Now the chamber was more illuminated and I could look about me once again and see as I had not seen for three days.

The priests stood around me and saw me not, they stood around a stone tomb resting in the center of the chamber. The chanting increased, and the ringing of the silver bells too. At last, at a signal given by an old man, six monks stopped and panting and grunting lifted the stone lid off the coffin. Inside as I looked down I saw my own body, a body clad in the robes of a priest of the lama class. The monks were chanting louder now, singing:

"Oh Spirit of the Visiting Lama, wandering the face of the world above, return for this, the third day, has come and is about to pass. A first stick of incense is lit to recall the Spirit of the Visiting Lama."

A monk stood forth and lit a stick of sweet smelling incense, red in color, and then took another from a box as the priests chanted:

"Oh Spirit of the Visiting Lama, returning here to us, hasten for the hour of your awakening draws nigh. A second stick of incense is lit to hasten your return."

As the monk solemnly drew a stick of incense from the box, the priest recited:

"Oh Spirit of the Visiting Lama, we await to reanimate and nourish your

26

earthly body. Speed you on your way for the hour is at hand, and with your return here another grade in your education will have been passed. A third stick of incense is lit at the call of returning."

As the smoke swirled lazily upwards engulfing my astral form, I shivered in dread. It was as if invisible hands were drawing me, as if hands were drawing on my Silver Cord, drawing me down, reeling me in, forcing me into that cold, lifeless body. I felt the coldness of death, I felt shivering in my limbs, I felt my astral sight grow dim, and then great gasps wracked my body which trembled uncontrollably. High Priests bent down into the stone tomb, lifted my head and my shoulders and forced something bitter between my tightly clenched jaws.

"Ah," I thought, "back in the confining body again, back in the confining body."

It seemed as if fire was coursing through my veins, veins which had been dormant for three days. Gradually the priests eased me out of the tomb, supporting me, lifting me, keeping me on my feet, walking me around in the stone chamber, kneeling before me, prostrating themselves at my feet, reciting their mantras, saying their prayers, and lighting their sticks of incense. They forced nourisment into me, washed me and dried me, and changed my robes.

With consciousness returning into the body, for some strange reason my thoughts wandered back to the time three days before when a similar occurrence had taken place. Then I had been laid down in this self same stone coffin. One by one the lamas had looked at me. Then they had put the lid upon the stone coffin and extinguished the sticks of incense. Solemnly they had departed up the stone corridor, bearing their lights with them, while I lay quite a little frightened in that stone tomb, frightened in spite of all my training, frightened in spite of knowing what was to happen. I had been long in the darkness, in the silence of death. Silence? No, for my perceptions had been trained, and were so acute that I could hear their breathing, sounds of life diminishing as they went away. I could hear the shuffling of their feet growing fainter and fainter, and then darkness, silence, and stillness, and nothingness.

Death itself could not be worse than this, I thought. Time crawled endlessly by as I lay there becoming colder and colder. All of a sudden the world exploded as in a golden flame, and I left the confines of the body, I left the blackness of the stone tomb, and the underground chamber. I forced my way through the earth, the icebound earth, and into the cold pure air, and away far

27

above the towering Himalayas, far out over the land and oceans, far away to the ends of the earth with the speed of thought. I wandered alone, ethereal, ghostlike in the astral, seeking out the places and palaces of the Earth, gaining education by watching others. Not even the most secret vaults were sealed to me, for I could wander as free as a thought to enter the Council Chambers of the world. The leaders of all lands passed before me in constant panorama, their thoughts naked to my probing eye.

"And now," I thought, as dizzily I stumbled to my feet supported by lamas, "Now I have to report all that I saw, all that I experienced, and then? Perhaps soon I shall have another similar experience to undergo. After that I shall have to journey into the Western world, to endure the hardship forecast."

With much training behind me, and much hardship too, I set out from Tibet to more training, and much more hardship. As I looked back, before crossing the Himalayas, I saw the early rays of the sun, peeping over the mountain ranges, touching the golden roofs of the Sacred Buildings and turning them into visions of breath-taking delight. The Valley of Lhasa seemed still asleep, and even the Prayer Flags nodded drowsily at their masts. By the Pargo Kaling I could just discern a yak-train, the traders, early risers like me, setting out for India while I turned towards Chungking.

Over the mountain ranges we went, taking the paths trodden by the traders bringing tea into Tibet, bricks of tea from China, tea which with tsampa was one of the staple foods eaten by Tibetans. 1927 it was when we left Lhasa, and made our way to Chotang, a little town on the river Brahmaputra. On we went to Kanting, down into the lowlands, through lush forests, through valleys steaming with dank vegetation, on we went suffering with our breathing, because we, all of us, were used to breathing air only at 15,000 feet or higher. The lowlands with their heavy atmosphere pressing upon us depressed our spirits, compressing our lungs, making us feel that we were drowning in air. On we went day after day, until after a thousand miles or more we reached the outskirts of the Chinese City Of Chungking.

Encamped for the night, our last night together, for on the morrow my companions would set off on the return journey to our beloved Lhasa, encamped together, we talked mournfully. It distressed me considerably that my comrades, my retainers, were already treating me as a person dead to the world, as a person condemned to live in the lowland cities. And so on the morrow I went to the University of Chungking, a University where almost all the professors, almost all the staff worked hard to ensure the success of the students, to help in any way possible, and only the very minute minority were difficult or un-coperative, or suffered from xenophobia.

In Chungking I studied to be a surgeon and a physician. I studied also to be an air pilot, for my life was mapped out, foretold in minutest detail, and I knew, as proved to be the case, that later I would do much in the air and in medicine. But in Chungking there were still only the mutterings of war to come and most of the people in this, an ancient and modern city combined, lived day by day enjoying their ordinary happiness, doing their ordinary tasks.

This was my first visit in the physical to one of the major cities, my first visit, in fact, to any city outside Lhasa, although in the astral form I had visited most of the great cities of the world, as anyone can if they will practice, for there is nothing difficult, nothing magical in the astral, it is as easy as walking, easier than riding a bicycle because on a bicycle one has to balance; in the astral one has merely to use the abilities and faculties which our birthright gave us.

While I was still studying at the University of Chungking I was summoned back to Lhasa because the Thirteenth Dalai Lama was about to die. I arrived there and took part in the ceremonies which followed His death, and then after attending to various business in Lhasa I again returned to Chungking. At a later interview with a Supreme Abbot, T'ai Shu, I was persuaded to accept a commission in the Chinese air force, and to go to Shanghai, a place which although I knew I had to visit had no attraction whatever for me. So once again I was uprooted and made my way to another home. Here on July 7th, 1937, the Japanese staged an incident at the Marco Polo Bridge. This was the actual starting point of the China-Japanese war, and it made things very difficult indeed for us. I had to leave my quite lucrative practice in Shanghai and place myself at the disposal of the Shanghai Municipal Council for a time, but afterwards I devoted all my time to mercy flying for the Chinese forces. I and others flew to places where there was a great need of urgent surgery. We flew in old aircraft which were actually condemned for anything else but which were considered good enough for those who were not fighting but patching up bodies.

I was captured by the Japanese, after being shot down, and they treated me quite roughly. I did not look like a Chinaman, they did not quite know what I looked like, and so because of my uniform, because of my rank, they were thoroughly unpleasant.

I managed to escape and made my way back to the Chinese forces in the hope of continuing with my work. First I was sent to Chungking to have a change of scene before returning to active duty. Chungking was then a different place from the Chungking which I had known before. The buildings were new, or rather some of the old buildings had new fronts because the place had been bombed. The place was absolutely crowded and all types of businesses from the major cities of China were now congregating in Chungking in the hopes of escaping the devastation of the war which was raging elsewhere.

After recovering somewhat I was sent down to the coast under the command of General Yo. I was appointed as medical officer in charge of the hospital, but the "hospital" was merely a collection of paddy fields which were thoroughly waterlogged. The Japanese soon came along and captured us and killed all those patients who were unable to rise and walk. I was taken off again and treated remarkably badly because the Japanese recognized me as one who had escaped before, and they really did not like people who escape.

After some time I was sent to be Prison Medical Officer in charge of a prison camp for women of all nationalities. There due to my specialized training in herbs, I was able to make the best use of the natural resources of the camp to treat patients who otherwise would have been denied all medication. The Japanese thought that I was doing too much for the prisoners and not letting them die enough, and so they sent me to a prison camp in Japan, a camp which they said was for terrorists. I was herded across the Sea of Japan in a leaky ship and we were very badly treated indeed. I was badly tortured by them, and their continual torture gave me pneumonia. They did not want me to die and so in their way they looked after me, and gave me treatment. When I was recovering—I did not let the Japanese know how well I was recovering—the earth shook; I thought it was an earthquake, and then I looked out of the window and found that the Japanese were running in terror, and all the sky turned red, it looked as if the sun was obscured. Although I did not know it, this was the atom bombing of Hiroshima, the day of the first bomb on October 6th, 1945.

The Japanese had no time for me, they needed all their time to look after themselves, I thought, and so I managed to pick up a uniform, a cap, and a pair of heavy sandals. Then I tottered out into the open air through the narrow unguarded doorway, and managed to make my way down to the shore where I found a fishing boat. Apparently the owner had fled in terror as the bomb dropped, for he was nowhere in sight. The boat idly rocked at its moorings. In the bottom there were a few pieces of stale fish already starting to give off the odor of decay. There was a discarded can nearby which had stale water in it, drinkable, but only just. I managed to hack away the flimsy rope holding the boat to the shore, and cast off. The wind filled out the ragged sail when I managed to hoist it hours later, and the boat headed out into the unknown. The effort was too much for me. I just toppled to the bottom in a dead faint.

A long time after, how long I cannot say, I can only judge the passage of time by the state of decomposition of the fish, I awakened to the dimness of a dawn. The boat was racing on, the little waves breaking over the bows. I was too ill with pneumonia to bale, and so I just had to lie with my shoulders and the bottom of my body in the salt water, in all the refuse which swilled about. Later in the day the sun came out with blinding power. I felt as if my brains were being boiled in my head, as if my eyes were being burned out. I felt as if my tongue was growing to be the size of my arm, dry, aching. My lips and my cheeks were cracked. The pain was too much for me. I felt that my lungs were bursting again, and I knew that once more pneumonia had attacked both lungs. The light of the day faded from me, and I sank back into the bilge water, unconscious.

Time had no meaning, time was just a series of red blurs, punctuated by darkness. Pain raged through me and I hovered at the border between life and death. Suddenly there was a violent jolt, and the screech of pebbles beneath the keel. The mast swayed as if it would snap, and the tattered rag of a sail fluttered madly in the stiff breeze. I slid forward in the bottom of the boat, unconscious amid the stinking, swirling water.

"Gee, Hank, dere's a gook in de bottom of de boat, sure looks like a stiff to me!" The nasal voice roused me to a flicker of consciousness. I lay there, unable to move, unable to show that I was still alive.

"Whatsamadder wid ya? Scairt of a corpse? We want da boat, don't we? Give me a hand and we toss him out."

Heavy footsteps rocked the boat, and threatened to crush my head.

"Man oh man!" said the first voice, "Dat poor guy he sure took a beating from exposure. Mebbe he still breathes, Hank, what ya think."

"Aw, stop bellyachin. He's good as dead. Toss him out. We got no time to waste"

Strong, harsh hands grabbed me by the feet and head. I was swung once, twice, and then let go and I sailed over the side of the boat to fall with a bone-rattling crash on to a pebble-and-sand beach. Without a backward glance, the two men heaved and strained at the stranded boat. Grunting and cursing they labored, throwing aside small rocks and stones. At last the boat broke free and with a grating scrunch floated slowly backwards into the water. In a panic, for some reason unknown to me, the two men scrambled frenziedly aboard and went off in a series of clumsy tacks.

31

The sun blazed on. Small creatures in the sand bit me, and I suffered the tortures of the damned. Gradually the day wore out, until at last the sun set, blood-red and threatening. Water lapped at my feet, crept up to my knees. Higher. With stupendous effort I crawled a few feet, digging my elbows into the sand, wriggling, struggling. Then oblivion.

Hours later, or it may have been days, I awakened to find the sunlight streaming in upon me. Shakily I turned my head and looked about. The surroundings were wholly unfamiliar. I was in a small one-roomed cottage, with sea sparkling and glistening in the distance. As I turned my head I saw an old Buddhist priest watching me. He smiled and came towards me, sitting on the floor by my side. Haltingly, and with some considerable difficulty, we con- versed. Our languages were similar but not identical, and with much effort, substituting and repeating words, we discussed the position.

"For some time," the priest said, "I have known that I would have a visitor of some eminence, one who had a great task in life. Although old, I have lingered on until my task was completed."

The room was very poor, very clean, and the old priest was obviously on the verge of starvation. He was emaciated and his hands shook with weakness and age. His faded, ancient robe was patterned with neat stitches where he had repaired the ravages of age and accidents.

"We saw you thrown from the boat," he said. "For long we thought you were dead and we could not get to the beach to make sure because of marauding bandits. At nightfall two men of the village went out and brought you here to me. But that was five days ago; you have been very ill indeed. We know that you will live to journey afar and life will be hard."

Hard! Why did everyone tell me so often that life would be hard? Did they think I liked it? Definitely it was hard, always had been, and I hated hardship as much as anyone.

"This is Najin," the priest continued. "We are on the outskirts. As soon as you are able, you will have to leave for my own death is near."

For two days I moved carefully around, trying to regain my strength, trying to pick up the threads of life again. I was weak, starved, and almost beyond caring whether I lived or died. A few old friends of the priest came to see me and suggested what I should do, and how I should travel. On the third morning as I awakened, I saw the old priest lying stiff and cold beside me. During the darkness he had relinquished his hold upon life, and had

32

departed. With the help of an old friend of his, we dug a grave and buried him. I wrapped what little food was left in a cloth, and with a stout stick to help me, I departed.

A mile or so and I was exhausted. My legs shook and my head seemed to spin, making my vision blurry. For a time I lay by the side of the coast road, keeping out of sight of passers-by, for I had been warned that this was a dangerous district indeed for strangers. Here, I was told, a man could lose his life if his expression did not please the armed thugs who roamed at large terrorizing the district.

Eventually I resumed my journey and made my way to Unggi. My informants had given me very clear instructions on how to cross the border into Russian territory. My condition was bad, frequent rests were necessary, and on one such occasion I was sitting by the side of the road idly watching the heavy traffic. My eyes wandered from group to group until I was attracted to five Russian soldiers, heavily armed and with three huge mastiffs. For some reason, at the same time, one of the soldiers chanced to look at me. With a word to his companions he unleashed the three dogs which came towards me in a blue of speed, their snarling fangs slavering with fierce excitement. The soldiers started towards me, fingering their sub-machine guns. As the dogs came, I sent friendly thoughts to them, animals had no fear or dislike of me. Suddenly they were upon me, tails wagging, licking and slobbering over me and nearly killing me with friendship, for I was very weak. A sharp command, and the dogs cowered at the feet of the soldiers, now standing over me. "Ah!" said the corporal in charge, "You must be a good Russian and a native here, otherwise the dogs would have torn you to pieces. They are trained for just that. Watch awhile and you will see."

They walked away, dragging the reluctant dogs, who wanted to stay with me. A few minutes later the dogs leaped urgently to their feet and dashed off to the undergrowth at the side of the road. There were horrible screams suddenly choked off by frothy bubbling. A rustling behind me, and as I turned, a bloody hand, bitten off at the wrist, was dropped at my feet while the dog stood there wagging his tail!

"Comrade," said the corporal, strolling over, "you must be loyal indeed for Serge to do that. We are going to our base at Kraskino. You are on the move, do you want a ride that far with five dead bodies?"

"Yes, Comrade corporal, I should be much obliged," I replied.

Leading the way, with the dogs walking beside me wagging their tails, he took me to a half track vehicle with a trailer attached. From one corner of the trailer a thin stream of blood ran to splash messily on the ground. Casually glancing in at the bodies piled there, he looked more intently at the feeble struggle of a dying man. Pulling out his revolver he shot him in the head, then reholstered his gun and walked off to the half track without a backward glance.

I was given a seat on the back of the half track. The soldiers were in a good mood, boasting that no foreigner ever crossed the Border when they were on duty, telling me that their platoon held the Red Star award for competency. I told them that I was making my way to Vladivostok to see the great city for the first time, and hoping I would have no difficulty with the language. "Aw!" guffawed the corporal. "We have a supply truck going there tomorrow, taking these dogs for a rest, because with too much human blood they get too savage so that even we cannot handle them. You have a way with them. Look after them for us and we will take you to Vladi tomorrow. You understand us, you will be understood everywhere in this district—this is not Moscow!"

So I, a confirmed hater of Communism, spent that night as a guest of the soldiers of the Russian Frontier Patrol. Wine, women and song were offered me, but I pleaded age and ill-health. With a good plain meal inside me, the best for a long, long time, I went to bed on the floor, and slept with an untroubled conscience.

In the morning we set out for Vladivostok, the corporal, one other rank, three dogs and me. And so, through the friendship of fierce animals, I got to Vladivostok without trouble, without walking, and with good food inside me.

Chapter Three

The road was dusty and full of holes. As we drove along we passed gangs of women in the charge of an armed overseer, filling up the deepest of the holes with stones and with anything at hand. As we passed, the soldiers with me yelled ribald remarks and made suggestive gestures.

We passed through a populated district and on, on until we came to grim buildings, which must have been a prison. The half-track swept on and into a cobbled courtyard. No one was in sight. The men looked about in consternation. Then, as the driver switched off the engine we became immediately aware of a tremendous clamour, the shouting of men and the fierce barking of dogs. We hurried towards the source of the sound, I with the soldiers. Passing through an open door set in a high stone wall we saw a strong fenced enclosure, which seemed to contain about fifty huge mastiffs.

Quickly a man on the edge of the crowd of soldiers outside the enclosure gabbled out his story. The dogs, with human bloodlust upon them had got out of hand and had killed and devoured two of their keepers. A sudden commotion, and as the crowd shifted and swayed, I saw a third man, clinging high up on the wire fence, lose his grip on the wire and fall among the dogs. There was a horrid scream, a really blood-chilling sound, and then nothing but a snarling mass of dogs.

The corporal turned to me, "Hey, you! You can control dogs." Then, turning to a soldier beside him, "Ask the Comrade Captain to come this way, say we have a man here who can control dogs."

As the soldier hurried off I nearly fainted with fright on the spot. Me? Why always me for the difficulties and dangers? Then as I looked at the dogs I thought, "Why not? These animals are not so fierce as Tibetan mastiffs, and these soldiers smell of fear to the dogs and so the dogs attack."

An arrogant-looking captain strode through the crowd, which parted respectfully before him. Stopping a few feet from me he looked me up and down, and a disdainful sneer passed over his face. "Faugh, corporal," he said haughtily, "What have we here? An ignorant native priest?"

"Comrade Captain," said the corporal, "This man was not attacked by our dogs, Serge bit off the hand of a frontier-crosser and gave it to him. Send him into the enclosure, Comrade Captain."

The captain frowned, shuffled his feet in the dust, and industriously bit his nails. At last he looked up. "Yes, I will do it," he said. "Moscow said that I must not shoot any more dogs, but they did not tell me what to do when the dogs had the blood-lust. This man, if he is killed, well, it was an accident. If he should live, though very unlikely, we will reward him" He turned and paced about, then stood looking at the dogs gnawing at the bones of the three keepers whom they had killed and eaten. Turning to the corporal, he said, "See to it, corporal, and if he succeeds, you are a sergeant." With that he hastened away.

For a time the corporal stood wide-eyed. "Me, a sergeant? Man" he said, turning to me, "You tame the dogs and every man of the Frontier Patrol will be your friend. Get in."

"Comrade corporal," I replied, "I should like the other three dogs to go in with me, they know me and they know these dogs."

"So it shall be," he answered, "Come with me and we will get them."

We turned and went out to the trailer of the half-track. I fondled the three dogs, letting them lick me, letting them put their smell on me. Then, with the three dogs jostling and bounding around me, I went to the barred entrance of the enclosure. Armed guards stood by in case any dog escaped. Quickly the gate was opened a trifle, and I was roughly thrust inside.

Dogs rushed at me from everywhere. The snapping jaws of "my" three discouraged most from coming too close to me, but one huge, ferocious beast, obviously the leader, sprang murderously at my throat. For that I was well prepared, and as I stepped aside I gave him a quick thrust in the throat, a judo (or karate as people now term it) thrust which killed him before he touched the ground. The body was covered with a seething, struggling mass of dogs - allmost before I could jump out of the way. The snarling and snapping noises were hideous.

For a few moments I waited, unarmed, defenceless, thinking only kind and friendly thoughts towards the dogs, telling them by thought that I was not afraid of them, that I was their master. Then they turned, and I had a moment of revulsion as I saw the bare skeleton of what had moments ago been the leader. The dogs turned towards me. I sat upon the ground and willed them to do the same. They crouched before me, in a half-circle, paws

36

outstretched, grinning, tongues lolling lazily, and tails sweeping from side to side.

I stood up, and called Serge to my side. Putting my hand on his head, I said loudly, "From now on, you, Serge, will be leader of all these dogs, and you will obey me and will see that they obey me."

From outside the enclosure came a spontaneous roar of applause. I had forgotten all about the soldiers! As I turned I saw that they were waving their hands in friendship. The captain, his face suffused with excitement, came close to the wire and yelled, "Bring out the bodies of the keepers or their skeletons." Grimly I walked to the first body, a shredded, bloody mass, with the chest bones bare of flesh. I took it by an arm and pulled, but the arm came off at the shoulder. Then I pulled the man by the head, with his entrails dragging along behind. There was a gasp of horror, and I saw that Serge was walking beside me, carrying the man's arm. Laboriously I removed all three bodies, or what was left of them. Then, really exhausted with the strain, I stepped to the gate and was let out.

The captain stood before me. "You stink!" he said. "Get cleaned of the filth of those bodies. You shall remain here for a month looking after the dogs. After a month they return to their patrols and you can go. You shall have the pay of a corporal." He turned to the corporal and said, "As promised, you are now a sergeant as from this moment." He turned and walked away, obviously quite delighted with the whole affair.

The sergeant beamed upon me. "You are a magic-maker! Never will I forget how you killed that dog. Never will I forget the sight of the captain hopping from foot to foot filming the whole affair. You have done a big thing for yourself. Last time we had a dog riot we lost six men and forty dogs. Moscow came down heavy on the captain's neck. Told him what would happen if he lost any more dogs. He will treat you good. You mess-in with us now. We don't ask questions. But come, you stink, as the captain said. Wash off all that filth. I always told Andrei he ate too much and smelled bad, now I have seen him in pieces I know I was right." I was so tired, so exhausted, that even such macabre humour as this did not shock me.

A group of men, corporals, in the mess hall, guffawed loudly and said something to the sergeant. He roared, and hastened over to me. "Haw! Haw! Comrade priest," he bellowed, eyes streaming with mirth. "They say that you have so much of Andrei's inside on your outside that you should have all his possessions now he is dead. He has no relatives. We are going to call you Comrade Corporal Andrei for as long as you are here. All that was his is now yours. And you won me many roubles when I bet on you in the enclosure. You are my friend."

Sergeant Boris was quite a good fellow at heart. Uncouth, rude in manner, and without any pretence of education, he still showed much friendship to me for securing his promotion-"I would have been a corporal all my life else," he said-and for the large number of roubles he had won on me. A number of men had been saying that I had not a chance in the dog enclosure. Boris had heard, and said, "My man is good. You should have seen him when we set the dogs on him. Didn't move. Sat like a statue. The dogs thought he was one of them. He will get that crowd straightened out. You'll see!"

"Bet on it, Boris?" cried one man.

"Take you three months to pay," said Boris. As a direct outcome, he had won about three and a half years' pay and was grateful.

That night, after a very ample supper, for the Border Patrol men lived well, I slept in a warm hut by the side of the dog enclosure. The mattress was well stuffed with dried esparto grass, and the men had obtained new blankets for me. I had every reason to be grateful for the training, which gave me such an understanding of animals' nature.

At first light I was dressed and went to see the dogs. I had been shown where their food was kept, and now I saw that they had a very good feed indeed. They clustered around me, tails awag, and every so often one would rear up and put his paws on my shoulders. At one such time I happened to look around, and there was the captain, outside of the wire of course, looking on. "Ah! Priest," he said, "I merely came to see why the dogs were so quiet. Feeding time was a time of madness and fights, with the keeper standing outside and throwing food in, with the dogs tearing at each other to get their share. I will ask you no questions, Priest. Give me your word to remain here for four to five weeks until the dogs all move out and you can have the run of the place and go to the city when you want to."

"Comrade Captain," I replied, "I will gladly give you my word to remain here until all these dogs leave. Then I will be on my way."

"Another matter, Priest," said the captain. "At the next feeding time I will bring my cine camera and take a film so that the Superiors can see how we keep our dogs in order. Go to the Quartermaster and draw a new corporal's uniform, and if you can find anyone to help you in the enclosure, get them to clean it thoroughly. If they are afraid, do it yourself."

38

"I will do it myself, Comrade Captain," I replied, "then the dogs will not be upset."

The captain nodded curtly, and marched off, obviously a very happy man that he could now show how he managed the blood-lusting dogs!

For three days I did not move more than a hundred yards from the dog enclosure. These men were "trigger happy" and thought nothing of shooting into the bushes "in case there should be spies hiding" as they put it.

For three days I rested, regaining my strength, and mixing with the men. Getting to know them, getting to know their habits. Andrei had been much the same size as me, so his clothes fitted reasonably well. Everything of his had to be washed and washed again, though, because he had not been noted for cleanliness. Many times the captain approached me, trying to engage me in conversation, but while he seemed genuinely interested and friendly enough, I had to remember my role of a simple priest who merely understood the Buddhist Scriptures-and dogs! He would sneer at religion, saying that there was no afterlife, no God, nothing but Father Stalin. I would quote Scriptures, never exceeding the knowledge that a poor village priest could be expected to have.

At one such discussion, Boris was present, leaning up against the dog compound idly chewing a sliver of grass. "Sergeant," exclaimed the captain in exasperation, "the Priest has never been out of his little village. Take him around and show him the City. Take him on patrol to Artem and to Razdol'noye. Show him life. He only knows about death, thinking that that is life." He spat on the ground, lit a contraband cigarette, and stalked away.

"Yes, come on, Priest, you have stayed with the dogs so long you are beginning to look like them. Though I must admit that you have them well-behaved now. And you did win for me a pile of money. I float on air with it, Priest, and must spend it before I die."

He led the way to a car, got in, and motioned for me to do the same. He started the engine, moved the gear lever, and let in the clutch. Off we went, bouncing on the rutted roads, roaring into the narrow streets of Vladivostok. Down by the harbour there were many ships, almost more ships than I had known existed in the world. "Look, Priest," said Boris, "those ships have captured goods. Goods which were going to be "lend-lease" from the Americans to some other country. They think the Japanese captured them, but we ship the cargoes over The Railway (the Trans-Siberian Railway) back to Moscow where the Party Bosses have what they think is first pick. We have first pick because we have an arrangement with the docks. We turn a blind eye on their doings while they turn a blind eye on ours. Have you ever had a watch, Priest?"

"No;" I replied, "I have owned very little in my life. I know the time by the position of the sun and the shadows."

"You must have a watch, Priest!" Boris speeded up the car and shortly we drew alongside a freighter moored to the dock side. The ship was streaked with red rust and sparkling with dried salt spray. The journey round the Golden Horn had been a hard and rough one. Cranes were swinging their long jibs, unloading the produce from different parts of the world. Men were shouting, gesticulating, manipulating cargo nets, and pulling on hawsers. Boris jumped out, dragging me with him, and rushed madly up the gangplank, still with me in tow.

"We want watches, Cap'n," he bawled at the first man in uniform. "Watches, for the arm."

A man with a more ornate uniform than the others appeared and motioned us to his cabin. "Watches, Cap'n," bawled Boris. "One for him and two for me. You want to come ashore, Cap'n? Good time ashore. Do what you like. Girls, get drunk, we not interfere. We want watches."

The captain smiled, and poured drinks. Boris drank his noisily, and I passed mine to him. "He no drink, Cap'n, he a Priest turned dog watcher, good dog watcher, too, good fellow," said Boris.

The captain went to a space beneath his bunk and drew out a box. Opening it, he displayed perhaps a dozen wrist watches. Almost quicker than the eye could see, Boris picked two gold ones, and without bothering to wind them, slipped one on each arm.

"Take a watch, Priest," commanded Boris.

I reached out and took a chromium one. "This is a better one, Priest," said the Captain. "This is a stainless steel, waterproof Omega, a far better watch"

"Thank you, Captain," I replied, "If you have no objection, I will have the one of your choice."

"Now I know you are crazed, Priest," said Boris, "a steel watch when you can have gold?"

I laughed and replied, "Steel is good enough for me, you are a sergeant, but I am only a very temporary corporal."

From the ship we went to the Trans-Siberian Railroad sidings. Work gangs were busily loading the trucks with the choicest goods from the ships. From here the trucks would leave for Moscow, some six thousand miles away. As we stood there, one train moved out. Two engines pulling a vast array of railroad cars, each engine with five wheels on each side. Giant things which were well kept and which were regarded almost as living creatures by the train crew.

Boris drove along beside the tracks. Guards were everywhere, from pits in the ground armed men scanned the undersides of the passing trains, looking for stowaways.

"You seem to be very afraid of anyone illegally riding the trains," I said, "this is a thing which I do not understand. What harm could it do to allow people to take a ride?"

"Priest," sadly replied Boris, "you have no knowledge of Life, just as the captain said. Enemies of the Party, saboteurs, and capitalist spies would try to steal into our cities. No honest Russian would want to travel unless so directed by his Commissar."

"But are there many trying to take rides? What do you do with them when you see them?"

"Do with them. Why, shoot them, of course! Not many stowaways just here, but tomorrow I am going to Artem and I will take you. There you will see how we deal with such subversive elements. The train crews, when they catch one, tie his hands, slip a rope round his neck, and throw him off. Makes a mess of the track, though, and encourages the wolves". Boris slumped in the driving seat, his eyes scanning the packed railroad cars trundling along. As if electrified, he sat bolt upright and jabbed the accelerator right down. The car leaped ahead and raced past the head of the train. Slamming on the brakes, Boris jumped out, grabbed his sub-machine-gun, and hid by the side of the car. Slowly the train rumbled by. I caught a glimpse of someone riding between two railroad coaches, and then there was the stuttering stammer of the sub-machine-gun. The body tumbled to the ground between the tracks. "Got him!" said Boris triumphantly, as he carefully cut another nick in the stock of his gun. "That makes fifty-three, Priest, fifty-three enemies of the State accounted for."

I turned away, sick at heart, and afraid to show it, for Boris would have shot me as easily as he had shot that man if he had known that I was not the village priest.

The train passed on, and Boris walked to the riddled, bleeding body. Turning it over with his foot he looked at the face, and said, "I recognize this as a railroad worker. He should not have been riding. Perhaps I should blow off his face so there will be no difficult questions." So saying, he put the muzzle of the gun near the face of the dead man and pulled the trigger. Leaving the now headless corpse, he returned to the car and we drove away.

"I have never been on a train, Boris," I said.

"Well," he replied, "tomorrow we will go to Artem by goods train and you can look around. I have some good friends there I want to meet now that I am a sergeant."

For long I had cherished the idea of stowing away aboard some ship and steaming off to America. I mentioned ship-stowaways to Boris.

"Boris," I said, "you spend all your time stopping people at the frontier and making sure there are no stowaways on the trains. Yet all these ships, anyone could walk aboard and stay."

Boris leaned back and roared with laughter. "Priest," he guffawed, "you must be a simpleton! The Water Guards board the ships a mile from the shore and they check all members of the crew. Then they seal all hatches and ventilators, and pour cyanide gas into the holds and other spaces, not forgetting the life-boats. They get a good bag of stiffs from reactionaries who do not know about this."

I felt very sick at the callous manner in which these men treated the whole affair as sport, and I hastily changed my mind about stowing aboard ship!

Here I was in Vladivostok, but I had my allotted task in life, and as the Prophecy had stated, I had to go first to America, then to England, and back to the North American continent. The problem was-how to get out of this part of the world. I determined to find out as much as possible about the Trans-Siberian Railway, where the checks and searches ended, and what happened at the Moscow end.

The next day I exercised and fed the dogs early, and with them well settled, I set out with Boris and three other Guards. We travelled some fifty miles to an outpost where the three Guards were to replace three others. All the way the men were chatting about how many "escapees" they had shot, and I picked up some useful information. I learned the point at which there were no more checks, I learned that if one was careful one could travel to the outskirts of Moscow without being caught.

Money was going to be the problem, that I could see. I made money by standing duty for other men, by treating their ills, and through the good offices of some of them, treating wealthy Party members in the city itself. Like others, I arranged to visit ships, and took my share of the spoils of new train loads. All my "bounty" was turned into roubles. I was preparing to cross Russia.

Nearly five weeks later the captain told me that the dogs were now going back to their patrol stations. A new Commissar was coming, and I must leave before he arrived. Where was I going? he asked. Knowing my man by now, I replied, "I will remain in Vladivostok, Comrade Captain. I like it here."

His face grew apprehensive. "You must leave, get right out of the district. Tomorrow."

"But Comrade Captain, I have nowhere to go, and no money," I answered.

"You shall be given roubles, food, clothing, and taken out of this district."

"Comrade Captain," I reiterated, "I have nowhere to go. I have worked hard here, and I want to stay in Vladivostok."

The captain was adamant "Tomorrow we send men to the very limit of our area, to the boundary of Voroshilov. You shall be taken there and left. I will give you a letter saying that you have helped us and you have gone there with our permission. Then the Voroshilov Police will not arrest you."

This was far better than I had hoped. I wanted to get to Voroshilov, because that was where I intended to board the train. I knew that if I could get to the other side of that city I should be fairly safe.

The next day, with a number of other men, I climbed aboard a fast troop-carrier and we roared up the road on the way to Voroshilov. This time I was wearing a good suit of clothes, and had a large rucksack stuffed with belongings. I also had a shoulder bag full of food. It gave me not a qualm to remember that the clothes I wore had been taken from a dead ship-jumper.

"Don't know where you are going, Priest," said Boris, "but the captain has said that he trained those dogs, so you had to leave. You can sleep at the outpost tonight, and be on your way in the morning."

That night I was unsettled. I was sick and tired of roaming from place to place. Sick and tired of living with Death nudging my elbow. It was utterly lonely living with these people who were so alien, so absolutely opposed to my peaceful way of living.

In the morning, after a good breakfast, I said good-bye to Boris and the others, shouldered my load, and set off. Mile after mile I covered, avoiding the main road, trying to circle Voroshilov. There was the roar of a speeding car behind me, the squeal of hastily-applied brakes and I found myself looking down the muzzle of a sub-machine-gun.

"Who are you? Where are you going?" snarled a scowling corporal.

"I am on my way to Voroshilov," I replied. "I have a letter here from Comrade Captain Vassily."

Snatching the letter from me, he tore it open, frowning in the concentration of reading. Then his face broke into a broad grin. "We have just come from Sergeant Boris," he said. "Get in, we will drive you to Voroshilov and let you off where you say."

This was a nuisance, I was trying to avoid the city! But I climbed into the patrol car and was speedily driven to Voroshilov. I alighted near the Police Headquarters, and as the car shot off into the garage, I walked smartly along, trying to cover as many miles as possible before nightfall. I planned to camp out near the Railroad and observe what happened for a night and day before climbing aboard.

Passenger trains were stopped and checked at Voroshilov, but the goods trains stopped just outside, possibly so that the local people should not see how many stowaways were killed. I watched and watched, and decided that my only hope was to get on a train just as it was pulling out.

On the night of the second day a very desirable train stopped. A train which my experience told me had many "lend-lease" cargoes aboard. This was not one to be missed, I thought, as I eased myself along the tracks, peering under, testing locked doors, opening those which were not locked. Every now and then a shot rang out, followed by the thud of a falling body. Dogs were not used here for fear that they would be killed by the wheels. I rolled in the dust, making myself as dirty as possible.

44

The guards came by, peering at the train, shouting to each other, flashing powerfull lamps. No one thought to look behind the train, and the train only engaged their attention. I, prone on the ground behind them, thought, "my dogs would be far more efficient than this. Dogs would soon have found me!"

The men, satisfied with their search, strolled off. I rolled sideways to the track and darted between the wheels of a railroad car. Quickly I climbed on to an axle and hitched a rope I had ready to a projecting lug. Fastening it to the other side, I drew myself up and tied myself to the bottom of the railroad car floor-in the only position, which would escape scrutiny. This I had planned for a month. The train started with a jerk which nearly dislodged me, and as I anticipated, a jeep with a spotlight came racing alongside, with armed guards peering at the axle-bars. I drew myself tighter to the floor, feeling as a naked man would before a convention of nuns! The jeep raced on, turned and came back, and passed out of my sight and life. The train rumbled on. For five or six miles I held grimly to my painful position, then convinced that the danger was over, I slowly eased myself out from the rope and managed to balance on one of the covers of the axles.

For a time I rested as best I could, getting feeling back into my cramped and aching limbs. Then slowly, cautiously, I edged myself along to the end of the railroad car and managed to grasp an iron bar. For perhaps half an hour I sat on the couplings, then drawing myself up on that swaying platform, I crept blindly around the end and on to the roof. It was quite dark now, except for the starlight. The moon had not yet risen, and I knew that I had to work fast to get inside a wagon before any prowling trainman saw me in the Siberian moonlight. On the roof I tied an end of the rope around me, passed the other end around the roof-rail, and slid cautiously down over the side, paying out the rope I held. Bumping and scraping along the rough edges, I soon managed to unlock the door with a key which I had obtained in Vladivostok for the purpose - one key fitted all the train locks. It proved to be fantastically difficult to slide the door open as I swung like a pendulum, but light of the first rays of the bright moon gave me that extra impetus, the door slid open and I crawled exhaustedly inside. Relinquishing the free end of the rope, I jerked and pulled until the whole length was in my hands. Shaking with utter exhaustion, I slid the door shut and dropped to the floor.

Two or three days later-one loses all count of time under such conditions-I felt the train slowing. Hurrying to the door, I opened it a crack and peered out. There was nothing to be seen except snow, so I rushed to the other side. Train guards were running along after a group of refugees. Obviously a big search was under way. Picking up my belongings, I dropped over the side and into the snow. Dodging and twisting between the wheels of the trucks I managed to completely confuse my snow-trail. While I was still at it, the train started to move, and I grabbed desperately at the nearest icy coupling. By great good fortune I managed to get my arms around one, and I hung there, feet dangling, until a sudden jolt enabled me to get my legs up as well.

Standing up, I found that I was at the end of a truck which was covered with a stiff, frozen tarpaulin. The knots were solid ice, the heavy canvas was like sheet iron. I stood upon the swaying, ice-covered couplings battling with the icy knots. I breathed upon them, hoping that they would soften, but my breath froze and made the ice thicker. I dragged the rope backwards and forwards against the metal of the truck side. Darkness was falling when the last frayed strand parted, and I was able, with immense effort, to prise up an edge of the canvas and crawl inside. Inside, as I fell to the floor, a man jumped at me, flailing a piece of sharp steel at my throat. Instinct and habit came to my rescue, and the man was soon nursing a broken arm and moaning. Two other men came at me, one with an iron bar and one with a broken jagged bottle. To one with my training, they presented no real problem, and they were soon disarmed. Here was the law of the jungle, the strongest man was king! Now that I had beaten them, they were my servants.

The wagon was full of grain which we ate just as it was. For drink we collected snow or sucked ice, which we broke from the tarpaulin. We could get no warmth, for there was nothing to burn, and the train crew would have seen the smoke. I could manage with the cold, but the man with the broken arm froze solid one night and we had to dump him over the side.

Siberia is not all snow, parts of it are mountainous, like the Canadian Rockies, and other parts are as green as Ireland. Now, though, we were troubled with snow, for this was the worst season in which to be travelling.

We found that the grain disturbed us badly, it caused us to swell up, and gave us severe dysentery, weakening us so much that we hardly cared whether we lived or died. At last the dysentery abated, and we suffered the sharp pangs of starvation. I lowered myself over the side with my rope and scraped the grease from the axle boxes. We ate that, retching horribly in the process.

The train rumbled on. Around the end of Lake Baykal, on to Omsk. Here, as I knew, it would be shunted and re-assembled, I should have to leave before reaching the city, and jump aboard another train which had been remade. There is no point in detailing all the trials and tribulations of the change of trains, but I, in company with a Russian and a Chinaman, managed to board a fast freight train to Moscow.

46

The train was in good condition. My carefully-preserved key opened a wagon and we clambered inside, hidden by the darkness of a moonless night. The wagon was very full, and we had to force our way in. There was no glimmer of light and we had no idea of the contents. A pleasant surprise awaited us in the morning. We were starving, and I saw that one corner of the wagon was stacked with Red Cross parcels which had apparently not reached their destination, but had been "liberated" by the Russians. Now we lived well. Chocolate, canned foods, canned milk, everything. We even found in a parcel a little stove with a supply of solid, smokeless fuel.

Investigating the bales, we found them to be full of clothing and articles which could have been looted from Shanghai stores. Cameras, binoculars, watches. We fitted ourselves out in good clothes, for ours were in a shocking state. Our greatest need was for water. We had to depend upon snow which we could scrape off ledges.

Four weeks and six thousand miles after I left Vladivostok, the train was approaching Noginsk, some thirty or forty miles from Moscow. The three of us held a discussion and decided that as the train crews were becoming active-we heard them walking across our roofs-we would be wise to leave. Very carefully we inspected each other to make sure that there was nothing suspicious about us, then we picked a very good supply of food and "treasures" with which to barter. The Chinaman went first, and as we slid the door shut after him, I heard rifle fire. Three or hours later the Russian dropped off, fellowed by me after a half-hour interval.

I plodded along in the dark, quite sure of my way, for the Russian, a native of Moscow who had been exiled in Siberia, had carefully coached us. By morning I had covered a good twenty miles, and my legs, so badly battered in prison camps, were troubling me greatly.

In an eating place I showed my papers as a corporal in the Frontier Guards. These were Andrel's; I had been told that I could have all his belongings, and no one had thought of adding "except his official papers and Identity Card". The waitress looked doubtful, and called a policeman who was standing outside. He came in and there was much discussion. No, I had no food ration card, I had inadvertently left it in Vladivostok, food regulations were not enforced for the Guards at Vladivostok. The policeman fiddled with my papers, and then said, "You will have to eat on the Black Market until you can get to the Food Bureau and obtain another Card. They will have to get in touch with Vladivostok first." With that he turned and walked away.

The waitress shrugged her shoulders. "Have what you like, Comrade, it will cost you five times the official price." She brought me some sour, black bread and some awful-looking and worse-tasting paste. She misunderstood my signs for "drink" and brought me some stuff, which almost made me pass out on the spot. One sip of it, and I thought I had been poisoned. One sip was enough, but the waitress even charged me for water while she slurped up the vile brew for which I had paid so much.

As I left the policeman was waiting. He fell into step as I walked along. "This is very irregular, Comrade, walking with a pack on your back. I wonder if I should not take you to the Station for interrogation. Have you a spare watch on you, Comrade, to make me forget my duty?"

Silently I fumbled in my pocket, and then I produced one of the watches I had taken from the train. The police-man took it, glanced at it, and said, "Moscow-straght ahead. Avoid the main thoroughfare and you will be all right." Then he turned and walked away.

I plodded along the side roads, keeping a good look-out for policemen who might demand watches. It seemed to me, from my own experience, that Russians had a simply dreadful craving for watches. Many of them could not tell the time, but the mere fact of having a watch seemed to satisfy them in some strange manner. An emaciated man tottering ahead of me suddenly swayed and fell on to his face in the gutter at the side of the road. Passers-by did not even glance at him, but went on their way. I made as if to go to him when an old man just behind me muttered, "Careful, Comrade stranger, if you go to him the police will think you are looting. He is dead anyway. Starvation. It happens to hundreds here every day."

Nodding my thanks, I walked straight on. "This is a terrible place," I thought, "with every man's hand against his fellows. It must be because they have no religion to guide them."

That night I slept behind the crumbling wall of a derelict Church. Slept, with about three hundred others for company. My rucksack was my pillow, and during the night I felt stealthy hands trying to unfasten the straps. A quick blow to the would-be thief's throat sent him gasping and reeling backwards, and I was not troubled again.

In the morning I bought food on the Government Black Market, for in Russia the Government runs the Black Market, and then continued on my way. The Russian on the train had told me to pose as a tourist and to hang a camera (taken from the train) around my neck. I had no film, and in those days hardly knew one side of the camera from the other.

48

Soon I found myself in the better part of Moscow, the part that the ordinary tourist sees, for the ordinary tourist does not see "behind the scenes", - the misery, poverty and death which exists in the slum side streets. The Moscow River was before me, and I walked along its banks for a time before turning up into Red Square. The Kremlin, and the Tomb of Lenin impressed me not at all. I was used to the grandeur and sparkling beauty of the Potala. Near an entrance to the Kremlin a small group of people waited, apathetic, slovenly, looking as if they had been driven there like cattle. With a "swoosh" three huge black cars rushed out, across the Square, and disappeared into the obscurity of the streets. As people were looking dully in my direction, I half-raised the camera. Suddenly I felt a terrific pain shoot through my head. For a moment I thought that a building had fallen on me. I fell to the ground, and the camera was smashed from my hands.

Towering Soviet guards stood over me; one of them was methodically and unemotionally kicking me in the ribs in order to make me rise to my feet. Half stunned as I was, it was difficult for me to rise, so two policemen reached down and roughly dragged me to my feet. They fired questions at me, but they spoke so rapidly and in such a "Moscow accent" that I understood not a word. At last, tired of asking questions and getting no reply, they marched me off along Red Square, a policeman on each side, and one behind me with a huge revolver poking painfully into my spine.

We stopped at a dismal looking building, and entered by a basement door. I was roughly pushed-shoved would be a better word-down some stone steps and into a small room. An officer was sitting at a table, with two armed guards standing by a wall of the room. The senior policeman in charge of me gabbled out a lengthy explanation to the officer, and placed my rucksack on the floor beside him. The officer wrote what was obviously a receipt for me and for my belongings, and then the policemen turned and left.

I was roughly pushed into another room, a very large one, and left standing before an immense desk, with an armed guard on each side of me. Some time later, three men came in and seated themselves at the desk and went through the contents of my rucksack. One rang for an attendant, and, when he entered, gave him my camera, giving him brusque instructions. The man turned, and went off, carefully carrying that inoffensive camera as if it were a bomb about to explode.

They kept on asking me questions, which I could not understand. At last, they called an interpreter, then another, and another until they found one who could converse with me. I was stripped of my clothes and examined by a doctor. All the seams of my clothing were examined, and some of them were

49

ripped open. At last my clothes were flung at me, less buttons, less belt and shoe laces. At a command the guards hustled me out of the room, carrying my clothes, and marched me along corridor after corridor. They made no sound, felt slippers were on their feet, nor did they speak to each other or to me. As we marched silently along, a really blood-curdling scream rose and fell quaveringly on the still air. I involuntarily slowed down, but the guard behind me jumped at my shoulder with such force that I thought he had broken my neck.

At last we stopped at a red door. A guard unlocked it, and I was pushed in to fall headlong down three stone steps. The cell was dark and very damp. It was about six feet by twelve feet, with a foul and stinking mattress on the floor. For a quite unknown time I stayed there in the dark-ness, becoming hungrier and hungrier, wondering why mankind had such a savage nature.

After a very long interval, a hunk of sour black bread and a small jug of brackish water was passed in. The silent guard motioned for me to drink the water then. I took a gulp, and he snatched the jug from my lips, poured the water on the floor, and went out. The door closed silently. There was no sound except occasional hideous screams, which were quickly and violently suppressed. Time crawled on. I nibbled at the sour black bread. I was hungry and thought that I could have eaten anything, but this bread was terrible; it stank as if it had been dragged through a cesspool.

A long time after, so long that I feared I was quite forgotten, armed guards came silently to my cell. Not a word was spoken; they gestured for me to go with them. Having no choice, I did so, and we tramped through endless corridors, giving me the impression that we were retracing our steps time after time in order to build up a suspense. At last I was marched into a long room which had a brightly painted white wall at one end. Roughly the guards manacled my arms behind me, and turned me to face the white wall. For long moments nothing happened, then very powerful, utterly dazzling lights were switched on so as to reflect from the white wall. It felt as if my eyeballs were being scorched even with my eyes shut. The guards wore dark glasses. The light beat down in waves. The sensation was as if needles were being pushed into my eyes.

A door softly opened and shut. The scrape of chairs and the rustle of papers. A low-voiced muttered conversation which I did not understand. Then-the blow of a rifle-butt between my shoulders, and the questioning began. Why had I a camera which had no flim in it? Why had I the papers of a Frontier Guard stationed at Vladivostok. How? Why? When? Hour after hour the same stupid questions. The light blazed on, giving me a splitting headache. A blow from a gun-butt if I refused to answer. The only respite was for a few moments every two hours when the guards and questioners were replaced by fresh ones; for the guards too became exhausted by the bright lights.

After what seemed to be endless hours, but which in reality could not have been more than six, I collapsed on the floor. Guards quite unemotionally began pricking me with their sharpened bayonets. To struggle to my feet with my arms fixed behind me was difficult, but I did it, again and again. When I became unconscious buckets of cesspool water were thrown over me. Hour after hour the questioning went on. My legs began to swell. My ankles became thicker than my thighs as the body fluids drained down and made the flesh waterlogged.

Always the same questions, always the same brutality. Sixty hours of standing. Seventy hours. The world was a red haze now, I was all but dead on my feet. No food, no rest, no respite. Just a drink of some sleep-preventing drug forced into my mouth. Questions. Questions. Questions. Seventy-two hours, and I heard no more, saw no more. The questions, the lights, the pain, all faded, and there was blackness.

An unspecified time elapsed, and I regained a pain-filled consciousness, flat on my back on the cold, wet floor of a reeking cell. It was agony to move, my flesh felt soggy and my back felt as if the spine were made of broken glass. No sound there was to show that others were alive, no glimmer of light to mark night from day. Nothing, but an eternity of pain, hunger and thirst. At last there was a chink of light as a guard roughly shoved a plate of food on to the floor. A can of water slopped beside it. The door shut, and again I was alone with my thoughts in the darkness.

Much later the guards came again, and I was dragged-I could not walk-to the Interrogation Room. There I had to sit and write my life history. For five days the same thing happened. I was taken to a room, given a pencil stub and paper and told to write everything about myself. For three weeks I remained in my cell, recovering slowly.

Once again I was taken to a room, where I stood before three high officials. One glanced at the others, looked at a paper in his hands, and told me that certain influential people had testified that I had helped people in Vladivostok. One testified that I had helped his daughter escape from a Japanese Prisoner of War camp.

"You will be released," said the official, "and taken to Stryj, in Poland. We have a detachment of men going there. You will accompany them."

Back to a cell-a better one this time-while my strength was built up enough to enable me to travel. At last I marched through the gate of the Lubianka Prison, Moscow, on my way to the West.

Chapter Four

OUTSIDE the Lubianka three soldiers were waiting. The prison guard who thrust me through the opened door handed a paper to the senior soldier, a corporal. "Sign here, Comrade, it is just to say you acknowledge receipt of a Deportee." The corporal dubiously scratched his head, licked the pencil and wiped his palms on his trouser legs before hesitatingly scribbling his name. The prison guard turned back without a word, and the Lubianka door slammed shut-fortunately this time with me on the outside.

The corporal scowled at me. "Now, through you, I have had to sign a paper. Lenin only knows what will happen, I might even end up in the Lubianka myself. Come on, get moving!"

The corporal took his place in front of me, and with a soldier on each side, I was marched through the streets of Moscow to a railway station. I had nothing to carry, every-thing I owned was upon me, my suit of clothes. The Russians had kept my rucksack, my watch, everything except the clothes which I actually wore. And those clothes? Heavy shoes with wooden soles, trousers, and a jacket. Nothing else. No underwear, no money, no food. Nothing. Yes, there was something! I had in my pocket a paper saying that I was deported from Russia and that I was free to make my way to Russian-occupied Germany where I should report to the nearest police station.

At the Moscow railway station we sat and waited in the freezing cold. One after the other the soldiers wandered off and returned so that another could go. I sat on the stone platform and shivered. I was hungry. I felt ill and weak. At long last a sergeant and about a hundred men appeared. The sergeant marched down the platform and took a look at me.

"Do you want him to die?" he bawled at the corporal.

"We have to deliver him alive at Lwow. See that he eats, we have six hours before the train leaves."

The corporal and an ordinary soldier each took one of my arms and dragged me to my feet. The sergeant looked me in the face and said, "H'mm. Not a bad sort of fellow. See you give us no trouble and we will cause you none." He looked at my papers, which the corporal was carrying. "My brother was in the Lubianka," he said, making sure that none of his men were within listening distance. "He did nothing either. They sent him to Siberia. Now I will have you taken for food. Eat well, for after we reach Lwow, you will be on your own." He turned away, and called two corporals. "Look after him, see he gets all the food and drink he wants, he has to leave us in good condition or the Commissar will say we kill prisoners."

Wearily I went off between the two corporals. At a little eating place outside the station the senior corporal ordered great bowls of cabbage soup and loaves of black bread. The stuff stank of decayed vegetation, but I managed to get it down, as I was so hungry. I thought of the "soup" we had had in the Japanese Prison Camps, where bits of gristle spat out by the Japanese, and food which they left was collected and made into "soup" for the prisoners.

With a meal inside us, we were ready to leave. A corporal ordered more bread and three copies of Pravda. We wrapped our bread in the papers, first being sure that we did not desecrate any pictures of Stalin in the process, and then returned to the railway station.

The wait was terrible. Six hours in the freezing cold, sitting on a stone platform. Eventually we were all herded into a weary old train, and set off for Kiev. That night I slept propped up between two snoring Russian soldiers. There was not room for any of us to lie down, we were crammed in very tightly. The hard wooden seats were uncomfortable, and I wished that I could sit on the floor. The train jolted on, coming to a creaky halt, so it seemed, every time I had just managed to go to sleep. Very late the following night, after a painful journey of some four hundred and eighty miles or so, we drew into a second-rate station at Kiev. There was much bustling, much shouting, and we all marched off to the local barracks for the night. I was shoved into a cell and after many hours I was awakened from my sleep by the entry of a Commissar and his assistant. They asked me questions, endless questions, and after perhaps two or two and a half hours, they went out again.

For some time I tossed and turned, trying to get to sleep. Violent hands smacked my face, shouting "wake up, wake up, are you dead? Here is food. Hurry - you have minutes only before you leave."

Food? More cabbage soup. More sour black bread, and water to drink. I gulped the stuff down, afraid that I should have to go before I had finished my miserable meal. Gulped it down, and waited. Waited hours. Late that afternoon two Military Policemen entered, questioned me all over again, took my fingerprints once more, and they said, "We are late. There is no time for you to have a meal now. You may be able to get something at the railway station.

54

Outside the barracks, three troop-carriers were waiting. Forty soldiers and I crammed unbelievably into one, the others climbed aboard the two other vehicles, and we were off, jolting dangerously along the road to the station. Jammed so tight that I could scarce breathe. The driver of our troop-carrier seemed to be mad, far outstripping the other two cars. He drove as if all the devils of Communism were after him. We swayed and jolted in the back, all of us standing as there was not room to sit. We caromed down the road in a frenzy of speed, there was the shrill squeal of brakes too hastily applied, and the carrier slithered sideways. The side in front of me ripped away in a shower of sparks as we collided with a thick stone wall. Screams, yells, and oaths, and a veritable sea of blood, and I found myself flying through the air. Flying, and I could see below me the wrecked carrier, now blazing furiously. A sensation of falling, a shattering crash, and blackness.

"Lobsang!" said a well-loved voice, the voice of my Guide, the Lama Mingyar Dondnp. "You are very ill, Lobsang, your body is still on Earth, but we have you here in a world beyond the Astral. We are trying to help you, because your task on Earth is not yet finished."

Mingyar Dondup? Ridiculous! He had been killed by the treacherous Communists when trying to arrange a peaceful settlement in Tibet. I had seen the dreadful wounds made when he was stabbed in the back. But of course, I had seen him several times since he had passed to the Heavenly Fields.

The light hurt my closed eyes. I thought that I was again facing that wallin the Lubianka Prison, and that the soldiers would again club me between the shoulders with their rifle-butts. But this light was different, it did not hurt my eyes; that must have been the association of ideas, I thought dully.

"Lobsang, open your eyes and look at me!" The kind voice of my Guide warmed me and sent a thrill of pleasure through my being. I opened my eyes and looked about me. Bending over me I saw the Lama. He was looking better than I had ever seen him on Earth. His face looked ageless, his aura was of the purest colours without trace of the passions of Earth people. His saffron robe was a material not of Earth, it positively glowed as if imbued with a life of of its own. He smiled down at me and said, "My poor Lobsang, Man's inhumanity to Man has indeed been exemplified in your case, because you have lived through that which would have killed others many times over. You are here for a rest, Lobsang. A rest in what we call 'The Land of the Golden Light'. Here we are beyond the stage of reincarnating. Here we work to help peoples of many different worlds, not merely that called Earth. Your soul is bruised and your body is shattered. We have to patch you up, Lobsang, for the task has to be done, and there is no substitute for you."

I looked about me and saw that I was in what appeared to be a hospital. From where I lay I could look out over beautiful parkland, in the distance I could see animals grazing, or at play. There seemed to be deer, and lions, and all those animals which could not live together in peace on Earth, here were friends who gambolled as members of one family.

A rasping tongue licked my right hand, which hung limply over the side of the bed. As I looked, I saw Sha-lu, the immense guard cat of the Chakpori, one of my first friends there. He winked at me, and I felt the goose-pimples start out all over me as he said, "Ah, my friend Lobsang, I am glad to see you again even for this short while. You will have to return to Earth for a time, after leaving here, then in a few short years you will return to us for always."

A cat talking? Telepathic cat talk I knew well, and fully understood, but this cat actually uttered words, not merely telepathic messages. Loud chuckles caused me to look up at my Guide, the Lama Mingyar Dondup. He really was enjoying himself-at my expense, I thought. My scalp prickled again; Sha-lu was standing on his hind legs by the bed, resting his elbows beside me. He and the Lama looked at me, then at each other; both chuckled. Both chuckled, I swear it!

"Lobsang," said my Guide, "you know there is no death, you know that upon leaving Earth at so-called 'death' the ego goes to that plane where he or she rests a while-before preparing to reincarnate in a body which will afford opportunities for learning other lessons and progressing ever upwards. Here we are in a plane from whence there is no reincarnating. Here we live, as you see us now, in harmony, at peace, and with the ability to go anywhere at any time by what you would call 'super-astral travelling'. Here animals and humans, and other species too, converse by speech as well as by telepathy. We use speech when close, and telepathy when distant."

In the distance I could hear soft music, music which even I could understand. My tutors at the Chakpori had lamented long over my inability to sing or make music. Their hearts would have been gladdened, I thought, if they could have seen how I enjoyed this music. Across the luminous sky colours flitted and wavered as if accompanying the music. Here, on this glorious landscape, the greens were greener, and the water bluer. Here were no trees gnarled by disease, no leaves with blight upon them. Here was only perfection. Perfection? Then what was I doing here? I was painfully far from perfect, as I well knew.

"You have fought the good fight, Lobsang, and you are here, for a holiday and to be encouraged, by right of attainment." My Guide smiled benevolently as he spoke.

I lay back, then started up in fright, "My body, where is my Earth body?"

"Rest, Lobsang, rest," replied the Lama. "Rest and we will show you much when your strength is greater."

Slowly the light in the room faded from golden to a restful purplish haze. I felt a cool, strong hand placed upon my forehead, and a soft, furry paw rested in the palm of my right hand, and I knew no more.

I dreamed that I was again upon Earth. I gazed down, emotionless while Russian soldiers raked through the ruined troop-carrier, pulling out burned bodies and bits of bodies. I saw a man look up, and point. Heads turned upwards in answer to his gestures, and I looked as well. There was my broken body teetering across the top of a high wall. Blood was running from the mouth and nostrils. I watched while my body was removed from the wall and placed in an ambulance. As the car drove off to a hospital I hovered above and saw all. My Silver Cord was intact, I observed; it glistened like blue morning mists in the valleys.

Russian orderlies pulled out the stretcher, not being particularly careful. Joltingly they carried it into an operating theatre and rolled my body on to a table. Nurses cut off my blood-stained clothes and dropped them in a refuse bin. An X-ray unit took photographs, and I saw that I had three broken ribs, one had perforated my left lung. My left arm was broken in two places, and my left leg was broken again at the knee and at the ankle. The broken end of a soldier's bayonet had penetrated my left shoulder, narrowly missing a vital artery. The women surgeons sighed noisily, wondering where to start. I seemed to float over the operating table, watching, wondering if their skill would be great enough to patch me up. A gentle tugging upon my Silver Cord, and I found myself floating up through the ceiling, seeing in my passing, patients in their beds in wards above. I drifted up and away, out into space, out among the limitless stars, beyond the astral, through etheric plane after plane, until I reached again the "Land of the Golden Light".

I started, trying to peer through the purple mist. "He has returned," a gentle voice said, and the mists receded, giving way to the glorious Light again. My Guide, the Lama Mingyar Dondup, stood beside me, looking down. Sha-lu was lying on the bed beside me, gently purring. Two other High Personages were in the room. When I saw them, they were looking out of the window watching the people strolling many feet below.

At my gasp of surprise they turned and smiled upon me. "You have been so very ill," said one, "we feared that your body would not endure."

The other, whom I knew well in spite of the exalted position he had had on Earth, took my hands between his. "You have suffered too much, Lobsang. The world has been too cruel to you. We have discussed this and feel that you may like to withdraw. There would be very much more suffering for you if you continued. You can abandon your body now and remain here through eternity. Would you prefer it so?"

My heart leaped within me. Peace after all my sufferings. Sufferings which, but for my hard and special training, would have ended my life years ago. Special training. Yes, for what? So that I could see the aura of people, so that I could influence thought in the direction of auric research. And if I gave up- who would continue that task? "The world has been too cruel to you. No blame will attach to you if you give up." I must think carefully here. No blame from others, but throughout eternity I would have to live with my conscience. What was life? Just a few years of misery. A few more years of hardship, suffering, misunderstanding, then, provided I had done all I could, my conscience would be at peace. For eternity.

"Honoured Sir," I replied, "you have given me my choice I will serve as long as my body will hold together. It is very shaky at this moment," I added. Happy smiles of approval broke out among the assembled men. Sha-lu purred loudly and gave me a gentle, playful bite of love.

"Your Earth body, as you say, is in a deplorable condition through hardship," said the Eminent Man. "Before you make a final decision, we must tell you this. We have located a body in the land of England, the owner of which is most anxious to leave. His aura has a fundamental harmonic of yours. Later, if conditions necessitate it, you can take over his body."

I nearly fell out of bed in horror. Me take over another body? My Guide laughed, "Now Lobsang, where is all your training? It is merely like taking over the robe of another. And at the passing of seven years the body would be yours, molecule for molecule yours, with the self-same scars to which you are so attached. At first it would be a little strange, as when you first wore Western clothes. I well remember that, Lobsang."

The Eminent Man broke in again, "you have your choice, my Lobsang. You can with a clear conscience relinquish your body now and remain here. But if you return to Earth, the time of the changing of bodies is not yet. Before you decide, I will tell you that if you return, you will return to hardship, misunderstanding, disbelief, and actual hatred, for there is a force of evil which tries to prevent all that is good in connection with human evolution. You will have evil forces with which to contend."

"My mind is made up," I replied. "You have given me my choice. I will continue until my task is done, and if I have to take over another body, well, so be it."

Heavy drowsiness assailed me. My eyes closed in spite of my efforts. The scene faded and I lapsed into unconsciousness.

The world seemed to be spinning round. There was a roaring in my ears, and a babble of voices. In some way that I could not explain, I seemed to be tied up. Was I in prison again? Had the Japanese caught me? Was my journey across Russia a dream, had I really been to the "Land of the Golden Light"?

"He is coming to," said a rough voice. "Hey! WAKE UP!" yelled someone in my ear. Drowsily I opened my aching eyes. A scowling Russian woman stared into my face. Beside her a fat woman doctor glanced stonily around the ward. Ward? I was in a ward with perhaps forty or fifty other men. Then the pain came on. My whole body came alive with flaming pain. Breathing was difficult. I could not move.

"Aw, he'll do," said the stony-faced doctor as she and the nurse turned and walked away. I lay panting, breath coming in short gasps because of the pain in my left side. No pain-relieving drugs here. Here one lived or died on one's own, neither expecting nor getting sympathy or relief from agony.

Heavy nurses stomped by, shaking the bed with the weight of their tread. Every morning callous fingers tore off the dressings and replaced them by others. For one's other needs, one had to depend on the good offices of those patients who were ambulant, and willing.

For two weeks I lay there, almost neglected by the nurses and medical staff getting what help I could from other patients, and suffering agonies when they could not or would not attend to my needs. At the end of two weeks the stony-faced woman doctor came, accompanied by the heavyweight nurse. Roughly they tore the plaster off my left arm and left leg. I had never seen any patient treated like this before, and when I showed signs of falling, the stalwart nurse supported me by my damaged left arm.

During the next week I hobbled round, helping patients as best I could. All I had to wear was a blanket, and I was wondering how I would get clothing. On the twenty-second day of my stay in the hospital two policemen came to the ward. Ripping off my blanket, they shoved a suit of clothes at me, and shouted, "Hurry, you are being deported. You should have left three weeks ago."

59

"But how could I leave when I was unconscious through no fault of mine?" I argued.

A blow across the face was the only answer. The second policeman loosened his revolver in its holster suggestively. They hustled me down the stairs and into the office of the Political Commissar.

"You did not tell us, when you were admitted, that you were being deported," he said angrily. "You have had treatment under false pretences and now you must pay for it."

"Comrade Commissar,' I replied, "I was brought here unconscious, and my injuries were caused by the bad driving of a Russian soldier. I have suffered much pain and loss through this."

The Commissar thoughtfully stroked his chin. "H'mm," he said, "how do you know all this if you were unconscious? I must look into the matter." He turned to the policeman and said, "Take him off and keep him in a cell in your police station until you hear from me."

Once again I was marched through crowded streets as an arrested man. At the police station my fingerprints were taken once more, and I was taken to a cell deep below the ground level. For a long time nothing happened, then a guard brought me cabbage soup, black bread and some very synthetic acorn coffee. The light in the corridor was kept on all the time, and there was no way of telling night from day, nor of marking the passing of the hours. Eventually I was taken to a room where a severe man shuffled his papers and peered at me over his glasses.

"You have been found guilty," he said, "of remaining in Russia after you had been sentenced to be deported. True, you were involved in an accident not of your making, but immediately you became conscious you should have drawn the attention of the Hospital Commissar to your position. In your treatment you have cost Russia much," he went on, "but Russia is merciful. You will work on the roads in Poland for twelve months to help pay for your treatment."

"But you should pay me," I answered hotly. "Through the fault of a Russian soldier I have been badly injured."

"The soldier is not here to defend himself. He was uninjured, so we shot him. Your sentence stands. Tomorrow you will be taken to Poland where you will work on the roads." A guard roughly grabbed my arm, and led me off to the cell again.

60

The next day I and two other men were taken from our cells and marched off to the railway station. For some time, in company with the police, we stood around. Then a platoon of soldiers appeared, and the policeman in charge of us went to the Sergeant in charge of the soldiers and presented a form to be signed. Once again we were in the custody of the Russian army!

Another long wait, and at long last we were marched off to a train which would eventually take us to Lwow in Poland.

Lwow was a drab place. The countryside was dotted with oil wells, the roads were terrible because of the heavy war traffic. Men and women worked on the roads, breaking stones, filling in holes, and trying to keep body and soul together on a starvation diet. The two men who had travelled from Kiev with me were very dissimilar. Jakob was a nasty-minded man who rushed to the guards with any tale he could trump up. Jozef was different altogether and could be relied upon to "pull his weight". Because my legs were bad and made it difficult for me to stand for long, I was given the job of sitting by the side of the road breaking stones. Apparently it was not considered that my damaged left arm and barely healed ribs and lungs were any drawback. For a month I stuck at it, slaving away for my food only. Even the women who worked were paid two zloty for each cubic yard of stone they broke. At the end of the month I collapsed, coughing blood. Jozef came to my aid as I lay by the roadside, ignoring the command of the guards. One of the soldiers raised his rifle and shot Jozef through the neck, fortunately missing any vital part. We lay by the side of the road together until a farmer came by in his horse-drawn cart. A guard stopped him and we were tumbled roughly on top of his load of flax. The guard jumped up beside him, and we trundled off to the prison hospital. For weeks I lay on the wooden planks that served as my bed, then the prison doctor said that I would have to moved out. I was dying, he said, and he would get into trouble if any more prisoners died that month, he had exceeded his quota!

There was an unusual consultation in my hospital cell. The prison Governor, the doctor, and a senior guard. "You will have to go to Stryi," said the Governor. "Things are not so strict, and the country is healthier."

"But Governor," I replied, "why should I have to move? I am in prison for no offence, for I have done no wrong at all. Why should I move and keep quiet about it? I will tell everyone I meet how it was arranged."

There was much shouting, much bickering, and at last, I , the prisoner, came up with a solution. "Governor," I said, "you want me out to save yourselves. I will not be shunted to another prison and keep quiet. If you want me to remain silent, let Jozef Kochino and I go to Stryi as free men. Give us clothes that we may be decent. Give us a little money that we buy food. We will remain silent and will go right away over the Carpathians."

The Governor grumbled and swore, and all the men rushed out of my cell. The next day the Governor came back and said that he had read my papers and saw that I was "a man of honor", as he put it, who had been jailed unjustly. He would do as I said.

For a week nothing happened, nothing more was said. At three o'clock on the morning of the eighth day a guard came into my cell, roughly awakened me, and told me I was wanted at "The Office". Quickly I dressed and followed the guard to the office. He opened the door and pushed me inside. A guard was sitting inside with two piles of clothing and two Russian army packs. Food was on a table. He motioned me to be silent and come to him.

"You are being taken to Styri," he wispered. "When you get there ask the guard-there will be one only-to drive you a little farther. If you can get him on a quiet road, overpower him, tie him up and leave him by the side of the road. You have helped me with my illness, so I will tell you that there is a plot to shoot you as you as escapees."

The door poened and Jozef came in. "Now eat your breakfast", said the guard, "and hurry up. Here is a sum of money to help you on your way". Quite a large sum it was, too. I could see the plot. The Prison Governor was going to say that we had robbed him and escaped.

With breakfast inside us, we went out to a car, a four-wheel-drive jeep type. A surly police driver sat at the wheel, revolver on the seat beside him. Curtly motioning to us to get in, he let in the clutch and shot out of the open gate. Thirty-five miles on our way-five miles from Styrj-I thought it was time to act. Quickly I reached over and did a little Judo push under the guard's nose, with the other hand taking the steering wheel. The guard toppled, foot hard on the accelerator. Hastily I switched off and steered the car to the side of the road. Jozef was watching open mouthed. Hastily I told him of the plot.

"Quick, Jozef," I said. "Off with your clothes and put on his. You will have to be the guard."

"But Lobsang," wailed Jozef, "I cannot drive, and you do not look like a Russian".

We pushed the guard out of the way and I got into the driver's seat, started the engine, and drove on until we reached a rutted lane. We drove along a little way and stopped. The guard was stirring now so we propped him up. I held the gun at his side.

"Guard," I exclaimed as fiercely as I could manage, "if you value your life you will do as I say. You will drive us around the outskirts of Strj and on to Skol'ye. There we will let you go".

"I will do anything you say," whimpered the guard, but if you are going to cross the Border, let me cross with you, or I shall be shot."

Jozef sat in the back of the jeep, carefully nursing the gun and looking with considerable longing at the back of the guard's neck. I sat by the driver, in case he should try any tricks such as running off the road, or throwing away the ignition key. We sped along, avoiding the main roads. The countryside became more hilly as we moved up into the Carpathian Mountains. The trees became denser, providing better hiding places. At a suitable spot we stopped to strech our legs and have some food, sharing what we had with the guard. At Vel'ke-Berezni, almost out of petrol, we stopped and hid the jeep. With the guard between us we moved steathily along. This was "Border country", and we had to be careful. Anyone who has sufficient reason can cross the border of any country. It merely calls for a little ingenuity and enterprise. I have never had the slightest real trouble in crossing a frontier illegally My only difficulties have been when I had a perfectly legitimate passport. Passports merely inconvience the innocent traveller, causing him to be subjected to ridiculous red tape. Lack of a passport has never hindered a person who had to cross frontiers. However, presumeably there have to be passports in order to harass harmless travellers and give work to hordes of often very unpleasant officials. This is not a treatise on how to cross frontiers illegally, so I will just say that without difficulty the three of us entered Czechoslovakia. The guard went his way, and we went ours.

"My home is at Levice," said Jozef, "I want to go home.You can stay with me as long as you like."

Together we made our way to Kosice, Zvolen, and on to Levice, walking, getting lifts, and riding on trains. Jozef knew the country well, knew where to get potatoes or beets or anything which could be eaten.

At long last, we walked up a mean street in Levice to a small house. Jozef knocked, and as there was no reply, knocked again. With extreme caution, a curtain was drawn aside an inch or so. The watcher saw and recognized Jozef. The door was flung open and he was dragged inside. The door slammed in my face. I paced up and down outside. Eventually the door opened again and Jozef came out looking more troubled than I had thought possible.

"My mother won't have you in," he said. "She says there are too many spies about and if we have anyone else in, we may all get arrested. I'm sorry." With that he turned shame-facedly away and re-entered the house.

For long moments I stood dazed. I had been responsible for getting Jozef out of prison, I had saved him getting shot. My efforts had brought him here, and now he had turned and left me to manage the best way I could. Sadly I turned and retraced my way down the street and on the long road again. No money, no food, no understanding of the language. I marched on blindly, saddened at the treachery of one I had called "friend".

For hour after hour I plodded along by the side of the highway. The few passing cars gave me not a glance, there were too many people "on the march" for me to attract attention. a few miles back I had assuaged my hunger somewhat by picking up some half-rotten tomatoes which a farmer had put out for his pigs. Drink was never a problem, for there were always the streams. Long ago I had learned that streams and brooks were safe, but rivers were polluted.

Far ahead of me on the straight road I saw a bulky object. In the distance it appeared to be a police truck, or road blockage. For several minutes I sat by the side of the road watching. There was no sign of police or soldiers, so I resumed my journey, being very cautious about it. As I drew near I saw that a man was trying to do something to the engine. He looked up at my approach and said something which I did not understand. He repeated it another language, and then in another. At last I could roughly understand what he was saying. The engine had stopped and he could not make it go, did I know about motors? I looked, and fiddled about, looked at the points, and tried the starter. There was ample petrol. Looking under the dash at the wiring I saw where the insulation had worn away, cutting off the ignition when the car had hit a bump in the road and jolted two bare wires together. I had no insulating tape or tools, but it was merely the work of moments to wrap the wires in strips of cloth and tie them safely. The engine started started and purred smoothly. "Something wrong here," I thought. "This engine goes too well to be an old farmer's car!".

The man was hopping up and down with joy. "Brava, brava", he kept exclaiming. "You have saved me!"

I looked at him in some puzzlement, how had I "saved him" by starting his car? He looked me over carefully.

"I have seen you before," he said. "You were with another man, and you were crossing the River Hron Bridge at Levice."

"Yes," I replied, "and now I am on my way alone."

He motioned for me to get into the car. As he drove along I told him about all that had happened. By his aura I could see that he was trustworthy and well-intentioned man.

"The war ended my profession," he said, and I have to live and support my family. You are good with cars and I can use a driver who will not get stuck on the road. We take foodstuffs and a few luxury articles from one country to another. All you have to do is to drive and maintain a car."

I looked very dubious. Smuggling? I had never done it in my life. The man looked at me and said, "No drugs, no weapons, nothing harmful. Food to keep people alive, and a few luxury articles for women to keep them happy."

It seemed peculiar to me, Czechoslovakia did not appear to be a country which could afford to export food and luxury goods. I said so, and the man replied, "You are perfectly correct, it all comes from another country, we merely forward it on. The Russians steal from the Occupied peoples, taking all their possessions. They put all the valuable goods on trains and send back loads of stuff to high party leaders. We merely intercept those trains which have the most good food which we can direct to other countries who are in need. All the Frontier Guards are in it. You would merely have to drive, with me beside you".

"Well," I said, "show me in this truck. If there are no drugs, nothing harmful, I will drive you wherever you wish".

He laughed and said, "Come on in the back. Look as much as you want. My regular driver is ill, and I thought I could manage this car myself. I cannot for I know nothing of mechanical things. I was a well-known lawyer in Vienna before the war put me out of work."

I rummaged, and turned out the back. As he said, there was only food and a few silk things which women wear. "I am satisfied," I said. "I will drive you."

He motioned me to the driver's, and we were off on a journey which took me through Bratislava, into Austria, through Vienna and Klagenfurt, and eventually into Italy, where the journey ended at Verona. Frontier Guards stopped us, made a show of inspecting the goods, then waved us on when a little package was placd in their hands. Once a police car raced ahead of us, stopped suddenly, and caused me to really stand on the brakes. Two policemen dashed at us with drawn revolvers. Then on production of certain papers, they backed away, looking very embarassed and muttering profuse apologies. My new employer seemed to be very pleased with me. "I can put you in touch with a man who runs trucks to Lausanne, in Switzerland," he said, "and if he is as satisfied as I am, he can pass you on to someone who will get you to Ludwigshafen in Germany."

For a week we lazed in Venice while our cargo was being unloaded and other goods put aboard. We also wanted a rest after the exhausting drive. Venice was a terrible place for me, I found it difficult to breathe in that lowland. It appeared to me that the place was merely an open sewer.

From Venice, in a different truck, we went on to Padua, Vicenza, and Verona. Among all the officials we were treated as public benefactors, and I wondered who my employer really was. From his aura, and the aura cannot lie, it was obvious he was a good man. I made no enquiries, as I was not really interested. All I wanted was to get going, to get on with my own task in life. As I knew, my task could not start until I could settle down, free from all this jumping from country to country.

My employer walked into my room in the Verona hotel. "I have a man I want you to meet. He is coming here this afternoon. Ah, Lobsang, you would do better if you shaved off your beard. Americans seem to dislike beards, and this man is an American who reconditions trucks and cars and moves them from country to country. Now about it?"

"Sir," I replied, "if the Americans or anyone else dislike my beard, they will have to go on disliking. My jaw bones were shattered by Japanese boots, and I wear a beard to disguise my injuries."

My employer talked with me for quite a time and before we parted he gave mea a very satifactory sum of money, saying that I had kept my side of the bargain, he would keep his.

The American was a flashy individual, rolling a huge cigar between his thick lips. His teeth were liberally studded with gold fillings, and his clothes really dazzled with their gaudiness. Dancing attendance upon him was a very artifically-blonde woman whose clothing scarce concealed those portions of her anatomy which Western convention decreed should be covered.

"Sa-ay," she squealed as she looked at me. Isn't he cute? Isn't he a doll?"

"Aw, shut it, Baby," said the man who provided her income. "Scram, go take a walk. We got business." With a pout and a jiggle that shook everything dangerously, and placed a heavy strain on flimsy fabric, "Baby" flounced out of the room in search of drinks.

"We gotta get a swell Mercedes out," said the American. "No sale for it here, it will fetch plenty money in another country. It used to belong to one of Musso's Big Shots. We liberated it and painted it over. I got a dandy contact in Karlsruhe, in Germany, if I can get it there, I stand to make a packet."

"Why do you not drive it yourself?" I asked. "I do not know Switzerland or Germany."

"Gee, me drive it? I have done it too often, all the Frontier Guards know me."

"So you want me to get caught?" I replied. "I have come too far too dangerously to get stopped now. No, I do not want this job."

"Aw, man! It's a cinch for you, you look honest and I can provide papers saying that it is your car and you are a tourist. Sure I can give you all the papers." He fished in a large brief-case which he was carrying, and shoved a whole sheaf of papers and forms at me. I idly glanced at them. Ship's engineer! I saw that they referred to a man, a ship's engineer. His union card and all were there. Ship's engineer! If I could get those papers I could get aboard a ship. I had studied engineering as well as medicine and surgery in Chungking; I had a B.Sc. in engineering, I was a fully qualified pilot...my mind raced on.

"Well, I am not keen on it." I said. "Too risky. These papers do not have my photograph on them. How do I know that the real owner will not turn up at the wrong moment?"

"The guy is dead, dead and buried. He got drunk and he was driving a Fiat at speed. Guess he fell asleep; anyhow he spattered himself along the side of a concrete bridge. We heard about him and picked up his papers."

"And if I agree, what will you pay me, and can I keep these papers? They will help me across the Atlantic."

"Sure, Bud, sure. I give you two-fifty bucks and all expenses, and you keep all the papers. We will get your photograph put on them instead of his. I got contacts. I fix it real good!"

67

"Very well," I replied, "I will drive the car to Karlsruhe for you."

"Take the girl along with you, she will be company and it will get her out of my hair. I gotta fresh one lined up."

For some moments I looked at him in a daze. He evidently mistook my expression. "Aw, sure, She's game for anything. You'll have plenty of fun."

"No!" I exclaimed, "I will not take that woman with me. I would not stay in the same car with her. If you distrust me, let us call it off, or you can send a man, or two men, but no woman."

He leaned back in his chair and roared, opening his mouth wide; the display of gold reminded me of the Golden Objects on display in Temples of Tibet. His cigar fell to the floor and became extinguished in a shower of sparks. "That dame," he said when he could finally speak, "she costs me five hundred bucks a week. I offer to give her to you for the trip and you refuse. Well, ain't that sump'n!"

Two days later the papers were ready. My photograph had been fixed on, and friendly officials had carefully examined the papers and covered them with official seals as necessary. The great Mercedes was gleaming in the Italian sunlight. I checked, as always, the fuel, oil and water, got in and started the engine. As I drove off the American gave me a friendly wave.

At the Swiss border, the officials very carefully inspected the papers which I presented. Then they turned their attention to the car. A probe into the fuel tank to make sure there was no false compartment, tapping along the body to make sure that nothing was hidden behind the metal panels. Two guards looked underneath, under the dash, and even looked at the engine. As they gave me clearance and I moved off, shouts broke out behind me. Quickly I braked. A guard ran up, panting. "Will you take a man to Martigny?" he asked. "He is in rather a hurry and has to go on a matter of some urgency."

"Yes," I replied, "I will take him if he is ready now."

The guard beckoned, and a man hurried out of the Frontier offices. Bowing to me, he got into the car and sat beside me. By his aura I saw that he was an official and was suspicious. Apparently he was wondering why I should be driving alone, with no woman friends.

He was a great talker, but he left time enough to ply me with questions. Questions which I could answer. "No women, Sir?" he said, "but how unusual. Perhaps you have other interests?"

I laughed and said, "You people think only of sex, you think that a man travelling alone is a freak, someone of whom you must be suspicious. I am a tourist, I am seeing the sights. I can see women anywhere.

He looked at me with some understanding in his eyes, and I said, "I will tell you a story, which I know, is true. It is another version of the Garden of Eden."

"Throughout history in all the great religious works of the world there have been stories which some have believed, but which others, with perhaps greater insight, have regarded as legends, as legends designed to conceal certain knowledge-which should not fall before any chance person because such knowledge can be dangerous in such hands.

"Such is the story or legend of Adam and Eve in the Garden of Eden, wherein Eve was tempted by a serpent and in which she ate the fruit from the Tree of Knowledge, and having been tempted by the serpent, and having eaten of the Tree of Knowledge, they gazed upon each other and saw that they were naked. Having obtained this forbidden knowledge, they were no longer allowed to remain in the Garden of Eden.

"The Garden of Eden, of course, is that blissful land of ignorance in which one fears nothing because one understands nothing, in which one is, to all intents and purposes, a cabbage. But here, then, is the more esoteric version of the story.

"Man and woman are not just merely a mass of protoplasm, of flesh stuck upon a bony framework. Man is, or can be, a much greater thing than that. Here on this Earth we are mere puppets of our Overself, that Overself which temporarily resides in the astral and which obtains experience through the flesh body which is the puppet, the instrument of the astral.

"Physiologists and others have dissected man's body, and they have reduced everything to a mass of flesh and bone. They can discuss this bone or that bone, they can discuss various organs, but these are all material things. They have not discovered, nor have they tried to discover, the more secret things, the intangible things, things which the Indians, the Chinese, and the Tibetans knew centuries and centuries before Christianity.

"The spine is a very important structure indeed. It houses the spinal cord, without which one is paralysed, without which one is useless as a human. But the spine is more important than that. Right in the centre of the spinal nerve, the spinal cord is a tube, which extends to another dimension. It is a tube

69

upon which the force known as the Kundalini can travel when awakened. At the base of the spine is what the Easterners call the Serpent Fire. It is the seat of Life itself.

"In the average Westerner this great force is dormant, asleep, almost paralysed with disuse. Actually it is like a serpent coiled at the base of the spine, a serpent of immense power, but which, for various reasons, cannot escape from its confines for the time being. This mythical figure of a serpent is known as the Kundalini, and in awakened Easterners, the serpent force can arise through the channel in the spinal nerve, rise straight up to the brain and beyond, beyond into the astral. As it rises its potent, force activates each of the chakrams, or centres of power, such as the umbilicus, throat, and various other parts. When those centres are awakened a person becomes vital, powerful, dominant.

"With complete control of the serpent force one can achieve almost anything. One can move mountains, or walk on water, or levitate, or allow oneself to be buried in the earth in a sealed chamber from which one would emerge alive at any specified time.

"So we have it in the legend that Eve was tempted by a serpent. In other words, in some way Eve got to know about the Kundalini. She was able to release the serpent power coiled at the base of her spine and that rose up and surged through the spinal column, and awakened her brain and gave her knowledge. Thus in the story it can be said that she ate of the Tree of Knowledge, or of the fruit thereof. She had this knowledge and with it she could see the aura, the force around the human body. She could see the aura of Adam, his thoughts and intentions, and Adam, too being tempted by Eve, had his Kundalini awakened and then he could see Eve as she was.

"The truth is that each gazed upon the aura of the other, seeing the other's naked astral form, the form unclothed by the human body, and so could see all the other's thoughts, all his desires, all his knowledge, and that should not be at the stage of evolution of Adam and Eve.

"Old priests knew that under certain conditions the aura could be seen, they knew that the Kundalini could be awakened by sex. So in the old days priests taught that sex was sinful, that sex was the root of all evil, and because Eve tempted Adam, sex was the downfall of the world. They taught this because sometimes, as I have said, sex can stir the Kundalini, which rests dormant in most people at the base of the spine.

"The Kundalini force is coiled down low, a terrific force, like a clock spring the way it is coiled. Like a clock spring suddenly uncoiled it can do damage. This particular force is located at the base of the spine, part of it actually within the generative organs. People of the East recognize this; certain of the Hindus use sex in their religious ceremonies. They use a different form of sex manifestation, and a different sex position to achieve specified results, and they do achieve those results. The ancients, centuries and centuries ago, worshipped sex. They went in for phallic worship. There were certain ceremonies in temples which raised the Kundalini which gave one clairvoyance, telepathy, and many other esoteric powers.

"Sex used properly and in a certain way in love, can raise one's vibrations. It can cause what the Easterners call the Flower of the Lotus to open, and to embrace the world of the spirit. It can cause the Kundalini to surge and to awaken certain centres. But sex and the Kundalini should never be abused. One should complement and supplement the other. Those religions which say that there should be no sex between husband and wife are tragically wrong. This is often advocated by many of the more dubious cults of Christianity. The Roman Catholics come nearer to the truth when they advise husband and wife to have sexual experiences, but the Catholics advocate it blindly, not knowing why, and believing that it is merely for the procreation of children, which is not the main purpose of sex, although most people believe it is.

"These religions, then, which say that one should have no sexual experiences-are trying to stifle individual evolution and the evolution of the race. This is how it works: In magnetism one obtains a powerful magnet by arranging the molecules of the substance to face in one direction. Normally in a piece of iron, for example, all the molecules are in any direction like an undisciplined crowd. They are haphazardly arranged, but when a certain force is applied (in the case of iron, a magnetizing force) all the molecules face in one direction, and so one has the great power of magnetism without which there would be no radio or electricity, without which there would be no road or rail transport, or air travel either.

"In the human, when the Kundalini is awakened, when the Serpent Fire becomes alive, then the molecules in the body all face in one direction because the Kundalini force, in awakening, has pulled the molecules in that direction. Then the human body becomes vibrant with life and health, it becomes powerful in knowledge, it can see all.

"There are various methods of awakening the Kundalini completely, but this should not be done except with those who are suitably evolved because of the immense power and domination of others which a complete awakening

71

would give, and power can be abused and used for ill. But the Kundalini can be partly awakened, and can vivify certain centres by love between a married couple. With the true ecstasy of intimacy, the molecules of the body become so arranged that many of them face in one direction, and so these people become people of great dynamic power.

"When all the false modesty and all the false teachings about sex are removed, then once again will Man arise as a great being, once again will Man be able to take his place as a traveller to the stars."

Chapter Five

The car droned on, surging with power that no mountainous pass could halt or impede my passenger sat silently by me, only occasionally speaking to point out landmarks of surpassing beauty. We approached the environs of Martigny and he spoke. "As an astute man like you will have guessed I am a Government official. Will you give me the pleasure of your company at dinner?"

"I should be delighted, sir," I replied. "I had intended to drive on to Aigle before stopping, but I will stay at this town instead."

We drove on, he directing me, until we arrived at a most excellent hotel. My luggage was carried in, I drove the car round to the garage and gave instructions for servicing.

Dinner was a most enjoyable meal, my ex-passenger, now host, was an interesting conversationalist, now that he had overcome his initial suspicion of me. On the old Tibetan principle that "He who listens most learns most," I let him do all the talking. He discussed Customs cases, and told me of a recent case where an expensive car had false panels behind which were stored narcotics. "I am an ordinary tourist," I said, "and one of the major dislikes in my life is drugs. Will you have my car examined to see if any false panels are in it? You have just told me of a case where they were installed without the owner's knowledge". At my insistence, the car was driven to the local Police headquarters and left overnight for them to examine. In the morning I was greeted as an old and trusted friend. They had examined every inch of the car and had found it to be innocent. The Swiss Police, I found, were courteous and affable, and very ready to assist a tourist.

I drove on, alone with my thoughts, wondering what the future had in store for me. More trouble and hardship, that I knew, for all the Seers had simply drummed that into me!. Behind me in the luggage compartment I had the luggage of a man whose papers I had taken over. He had no known relatives, like me he seemed to have been alone in the world. In his—or mine, now—cases he had a few books on marine engineering. I stopped the car, and took out the Manual. As I drove I recited to myself various rules which, as a Ship's Engineer, I should have to know. I planned to get a ship of a different Line;the Discharge Book would show me which Lines to avoid for fear of being recognized.

The miles reeled out beneath me. Aigle, Lausanne, and across the frontier into Germany. The German Frontier Guards were very thorough, checking everything, even engine and tire numbers. They were also completely humorless and dour.

On and on I drove. At Karlsruhe I went to the address which I had been given and was told that the man whom I was to see was at Ludwigshafen. So on I drove to Ludwigshafen and there, at the best hotel, I found the American. "Aw, Gee Bud," he said, "I could not take that auto over the mountain roads, my nerves are bad. Too much booze, I guess." I "guessed" so, too. His room at the hotel was like a remarkably well-equipped bar, complete with barmaid! This one had more to show, and showed more, than the one he had left in Italy. She had just three thoughts in her head, German marks, drink, and sex, in that order. The American was very pleased with the condition of the car, not a scratch and spotlessly clean. He marked his appreciation by a substantial gift of American dollars.

For three months I worked for him, driving immense trucks to various cities and bringing back cars which had to be reconditioned or rebuilt. I did not know what it was all about, I still do not, but I was well paid, and I was having time to study my marine engineering books. In the various cities I visited the local museums and carefully examined all the ship models, and models of ship engines.

Three months later the American came to the poor little room I had rented, and flopped down on my bed, reeking cigar fairly stinking out the place. "Gee, Bud," he said. "You sure don't go in for luxury! A U.S. prison cell is more comfortable than this. I gotta job for you, a big job. Want it?"

"If it will get me nearer the sea, to Le Havre or Cherbourg," I said.

"Well, this will take you to Verdun and it is quite legitimate. I gotta rig with more wheels than a caterpillar has legs. It's a crazy thing to drive. There's a lot of dollars in it."

"Tell me more about it," I answered. "I told you I could drive anything. Have you got clearance papers for it to enter France?"

"Yep," he said. "Been waiting three months to get them. We have been keeping you on ice and letting you earn some pocket money. Guess I never thought you were living in a dump like this, though."

He got up and motioned for me to follow him out. At the door he had his car, complete with girl-friend. "You drive," he said, getting in the back with the woman. "I will direct you." At what appeared to be an abandoned

airfield outside Ludwigshafen we stopped. There, in a huge shed, was the weirdest machine that I had ever seen. It seemed to be mainly yellow girders supported on a whole series of eight-foot wheels. Ridiculously high off the ground was a small glassed-in enclosure. Fixed on the back of the contraption were a whole series of lattice girders, and an immense steel scoop. Gingerly I climbed up to the seat. "Sa-ay," yelled the American, "Don't you want the handbook?" He reached up, and passed me a Manual dealing with these contraptions. "I had a guy," he said, "who was delivering a street sweeping truck, a new one. He would not read the book and when he got to his destination he found that he had had the brushes sweeping all the time and he had worn them out. I don't want you wrecking the road from here to Verdun,"

Fingering through the book I soon had the engine running. It made a roar like a plane taking off. Gingerly I let in the clutch and the mammoth machine lumbered out of the shed and on to what had once been a runway. I drove up and down a few times to become accustomed to the machine's controls, and as I turned to go back to the shed a German Police car drove up. A policeman got out, a savage looking fellow who appeared as if he had just shed the Gestapo badge. "You are driving that without an attendant," he barked.

"Attendant?" I thought, "Does he think I need a keeper?" I drove up alongside him. "Well, what is the trouble with you?" I shouted. "This is private property. Get off!" To my utter surprise he did! He got in his car and just drove outside the grounds.

The American walked over to him. "What's biting you, Bud?" he said.

"I have come to tell you that that machine can only be driven on the roads when accompanied by an attendant on the back to watch for overtaking traffic. It can only be driven at night, unless you have a police car at front and rear." For a moment I thought he was going to say "Heil, Hitler." Then he turned, got in his car and drove off.

"Gee," said the American. "That sure beats cockfighting. It sure do! I got a German named Ludvig who..."

"Not for me," I exclaimed fervently. "Not a German, they are too stodgy for me."

"Okay, Bud, okay. So no Kraut. Take it easy, don't get riled up. I got a Frenchie who you'll like. Marcel. C'mon. We will go see him." I parked the machine in the shed, looked over it to see that everything was shut off, and sauntered out, locking the door. "Don't you ever get rattled?" said the American. "Guess you better drive us."

Marcel had to be fished out of a bar. At first sight of him I thought his face had been stepped on by a horse. A second glance convinced me that his face would have been better if he had been stepped on by a horse. Marcel was ugly. Painfully ugly, but there was something about him which made me like him on sight. For some time we sat in the car discussing terms, then I returned to the machine to drive it and so become accustomed to it. As I lumbered round the track I saw a battered old car drive up. Marcel jumped out, waving frantically. I eased the machine to a standstill beside him. "I've got it, I've got it," he cried, all excitement. With much gesticulation he turned to his car—and nearly brained himself on the low- roofed door. Rubbing his head, and muttering fearsome imprecations against the makers of small cars, he rummaged on the back seat and came out with a large parcel. "Intercom," he shouted. He always shouted, even when standing just a few inches from one. "Intercom, we talk, yes? You there, me here, wire between, we talk all time. Good?" Shouting away at the top of his voice, he jumped on to the Earthmover, trailing wires and bits all over the place. "You want headset, no?" he yelled. "You hear me so much better. Me. I have mike." From the uproar he was making, I came to the conclusion that no intercom was necessary. His voice carried well above the throbbing of the mighty engine.

I drove along again, practicing turns, getting used to the thing. Marcel pranced and chattered from front to rear of the machine, twisting the wires around the girders. Coming to my "conning tower" he thrust an arm through the open window, thumped me on the shoulder, and bellowed, "The headset, you put her on, yes? You hear so good. Wait I go back!" He scuttled along the girders, plonked into his seat at the far end of the machine, and shrieked into the microphone. "You hear good? Yes? I come!" In his exuberance he had forgotten that I too had a microphone. Almost before I could collect my wits he was back, hammering at the window, "Good? Good? You hear good?"

"Say," said the American. "You guys take off tonight. All the papers are here. Marcel knows how to get you to

Paris, with the chance of earning francs on the way. Sure been nice knowing you." The American walked away, out of my life. Perhaps he will read this and get in touch with me through the publishers. I went off to my solitary

76

room. Marcel went off to the local place of refreshment. For the rest of the day I slept.

With the coming of darkness I had a meal and took a cab out to the shed. My luggage, now reduced to a bare minimum, I stowed in the space behind my seat. Engine started, pressures satisfactory. Fuel gauge reading Full. Lights working normally. I trundled the machine out in the open and drove around the track to warm it up. The moon rose higher and higher. No sign of Marcel. With the engine off I got out and walked around. At long last a car drove into the grounds, and Marcel got out. "Party," he roared. "Farewell party. We go now, yes?"

Disgustedly I restarted the engine, switched on the powerful lights, and rolled out into the road. Marcel was yelling so much that I just put the earphones around my neck and forgot all about him. Miles farther on a German police car pulled to a halt in front of me. "Your look-out is asleep. You are breaking Regulations by driving without a man keeping watch behind." Marcel came bounding up, "Me? Asleep? You do not see straight, Policeman. Because I sit in comfort you become officious." The policeman came closer and smelled my breath carefully. "No, he is a saint," said Marcel. "He does not take drink. Nor women," he added as an afterthought.

"Your papers!" said the policeman. Carefully he examined them, looking for any excuse to make trouble. Then he saw my American Ships' Engineer papers. "So. You are an American? Well, we want no trouble with your Consul. On your way." Pushing back the papers as if they were contaminated with the plague, he hurried back to his car and sped away. Telling Marcel what I thought of him, I sent him back to his seat, and we drove on through the night. At twenty miles an hour, the speed at which we were instructed to travel, the seventy miles to the French border seemed endless. Just short of Saarbrucken we stopped, pulled off the road so as not to impede traffic, and prepared to spend the day. After a meal I took our papers and went to the local police station in order to obtain clearance across the border. With a police motor cyclist at front and rear, we crept along side roads until we reached the Customs post.

Marcel was in his element talking to his French compatriots. I gathered that he and one of the Customs men whom he had met in "the Resistance" had, almost alone, won the war! With our papers checked, we were allowed to move into French territory. The friendly Customs man took Marcel off for the day, and I curled up beside the girders of the machine and went to sleep.

Very, very late indeed Marcel returned in charge of two French policemen.

With a wink at me, they strapped him in his seat, dead to the world, and cheerily waved me on my way. I roared on into the darkness, a mighty machine beneath me, a drunken "lookout" behind me. The whole time I kept careful watch for any prowling police cars. One came whizzing up, a policeman leaned out of his window, made a derisory gesture towards Marcel, waved his hand in greeting—and whizzed on.

With Metz well behind me, and no sign of life from Marcel, I pulled into the side of the road, got out and walked behind to look at him. He was fast asleep. No amount of shaking would rouse him, so I drove on again. As dawn was breaking I drove through the streets of Verdun, on, and into the large car park which was my destination.

"Lobsang", called a sleepy voice from the back. "If you don't get started we shall be late."

"Late?" I said. "We are at Verdun!"

There was a dead silence. Then an explosive "Verdun?"

"Listen, Marcel," I said. "You were brought to me drunk and incapable. You were strapped in your seat. I had to do all the work, I had to find my way. Now you get going and bring me breakfast. Get moving." A very chastened Marcel tottered off down the street to eventually return with breakfast.

Five hours later a short swarthy man drove up in an old Renault. Not a word to us, he walked round the Earthmover, carefully inspecting it, looking for scratches, looking for anything at which to complain. His thick eyebrows met like a bar across the bridge of his nose, a nose which had been broken at some time and badly set. At last he came up to us. "Which of you is the driver?"

"I am," I said.

"You will take this back to Metz," he said.

"No," was my answer, "I have been paid to bring it here. All the papers are made out for here. I have finished with it."

His face flushed with rage, and to my consternation he drew from his pocket a spring-loaded knife. I was easily able to disarm him, the knife flew over my shoulder, and the swarthy man was flat on his back. To my surprise, as I looked around, I saw that quite a crowd of workmen had arrived. "He's

78

thrown the Boss," said one; "He must have been taken by surprise," muttered another. Violently the swarthy man erupted from the ground, like a rubber ball bouncing. Dashing into the workshop he picked up a steel bar with a claw on the end, a bar used for opening packing cases. Rushing out, yelling oaths, he swung at me, trying to rip my throat. I fell to my knees and grabbed his knees and pushed. He screamed horribly, and fell to the ground with his left leg broken. The steel bar left his nerveless hand, skidded along the ground, and clanged against metal somewhere.

"Well, Boss," I said, as I rose to my feet. "You are not Boss of me, eh? Now apologize nicely, or I will beat you up some more. You tried to murder me."

"Get a doctor, get a doctor," he groaned, "I'm dying."

"Apologize first," I said fiercely, "or you will want an undertaker."

"What's going on here? Eh? What is it?" Two French policemen pushed into the throng, looked at "the Boss" on the ground, and laughed uproariously. "Haw! Haw!" roared one. "So he has met a better man at last! This is worth all the trouble we have had with him." The policemen looked at me with respect, and then demanded to see my papers. Satisfied on that point, and having heard the reports of the bystanders, they turned and walked away. The ex-Boss apologized, tears of mortification in his eyes, then I knelt beside him, set his leg, and fixed two boards from a packing case as a splint. Marcel had disappeared. He had run from trouble and out of my life.

My two suitcases were heavy. Taking them from the Earthmover I walked out into the street on another stage of my journey. I had no job and knew no one. Marcel had proved to be a broken reed with his brains pickled in drink. Verdun did not attract me at all at that moment. I stopped passer-by after passer-by for directions on how to get to the railway station so that I could leave my suitcases. Everyone seemed to think that I would be better off looking at the battlefields than looking for a station, but eventually I succeeded in obtaining the directions. Along the Rue Poincare I plodded, resting every so often and wondering what I could throw away to lighten my cases. Books? No, I had to keep those very carefully. Merchant Navy uniforms? Definitely a "must". Reluctantly I came to the conclusion that I had only essentials with me. On to the Place Chevert I trudged. Turning right I arrived at the Quai de la Republique. Looking at the traffic on the River Meuse and wondering about ships I decided to sit a while and rest. A large Citroen slid silently along, slowed up, and finally stopped by me. A tall, dark-haired man looked at me for some moments and then got out. Walking towards me, he said, "You are the man who earned our gratitude by beating up The Boss"

"I am," I replied. "Does he want some more?"

The man laughed and answered, "For years he has terrorized the district, even the police were afraid of him. He did great things in the war, he says. Now, do you want a job?"

I looked the man over carefully before replying. "Yes I do," I answered, "if it is legitimate!"

"The job I have to offer is very legitimate." He paused and smiled at me. "You see, I know all about you. Marcel was instructed to bring you to me, but he ran away. I know of your Russian journey and of your travels since. Marcel delivered a letter from 'the American' about you and then ran off from me as he did from you." What a network, I thought. However, I consoled myself, these Europeans did things in a manner different from us of the East.

The man motioned to me. "Put your cases in the car and I will take you off to lunch so that we may talk." This was sense indeed. At least it would get those horrid cases off my hands for a time. Gladly I put them in the luggage compartment and then got into the seat beside him. He drove off to the best hotel, the du Coq Hardi, where he was very obviously well known. With many exclamations at my modest requirements in the refreshment line, he came to the point.

"There are two elderly ladies, one of eighty-four and the other of seventy-nine," he told me, looking carefully around. "They are most anxious to go to the son of one of them who is living in Paris. They, are afraid of bandits — old people have such fears, and they have been through two severe wars— and they want a capable man who is able to protect them. They can pay well."

Women? Old women? Better than young ones, I thought. But I still did not like the idea much. Then I considered my heavy cases. Considered how I was going to get to Paris. "They are generous old ladies," said the man. "There is only one drawback. You must not exceed thirty five miles an hour." Cautiously I glanced round the big room. Two old ladies! Sitting three tables away. "Holy Buddha's Tooth," I said to myself. "What have I come to?" A picture of those suitcases rose before my mind's eye. Heavy cases, cases that I could not lighten. Money, too, the more money I had the easier I would live in America while looking for a job. I sighed dolefully, and said, "They pay well, you said. And how about the car? I am not coming back this way."

"Yes, my friend, they pay exceedingly well. The Countess is a wealthy woman. The car? She is taking a new Fiat to her son as a gift. Come—meet them." He rose and led the way to the two old ladies. Bowing so low that I was reminded of a pilgrim in the Holy Way in Lhasa, he introduced me. The Countess looked at me haughtily through her lorgnette.

"So you consider yourself to be capable of driving us safely, my man?"

I looked at her equally haughtily and replied, "Madam, I am not 'your man'. As to the question of safety, my life is as valuable to me as yours evidently is to you. I have been asked to discuss this driving matter with you, but I confess that now I have my doubts."

For long moments she stared icily at me, then the stony rigidity of her jaws relaxed, and she broke into quite a girlish laugh. "Ah!" she exclaimed, "I do like a bit of spirit. It is so rare in these difficult days. When can we start?"

"We have not discussed terms yet, nor have I seen your car. When do you want to go, if I agree? And why do you want me to drive? Surely there are plenty of Frenchmen willing to drive?"

The terms she offered were generous, the reasons she gave were good. "I prefer a bold man, a man of spirit, one who has been places and seen life. When do we leave? As soon as you are ready."

Two days I gave them, then we started out in a de-luxe Fiat. We cruised along the road to Reims, about eighty miles away, and there we spent the night. Dawdling along at thirty to thirty five miles an hour gave me time to see the countryside and to collect my thoughts which had hardly time to catch up with my travels. On the following day we started at midday and arrived in Paris in time for tea. At her son's house in the suburbs I garaged the car, and started off again with my two suitcases. That night I slept in a cheap Paris lodging house. The next day I looked about for anything that would take me to Cherbourg or Le Havre.

Car dealers were my first choice; did anyone want a car delivered in Cherbourg or Le Havre? I trudged miles, from dealer to dealer. No, no one wanted my services. At the end of the day I went back to that cheap little lodging house and walked into a scene of trouble. A man was being carried in by a policeman and another lodger. A wrecked bicycle, the front wheel completely twisted, lay at the side of the road. The man, coming home from work had looked behind over his shoulder, his front wheel had caught in a drain, and he was flung over the handlebars. His right ankle was badly sprained. "I shall lose my job, I shall lose my job," he was moaning. "I have to go to Caen on a furniture delivery tomorrow."

Caen? The name was vaguely familiar. Caen? I looked it up. A town some hundred and twenty-five miles from Paris and on the way to Cherbourg, it was roughly seventy five miles from Cherbourg. I thought it over and went to him.

"I want to get to Cherbourg or Le Havre," I said. "I will go on the furniture van and do your job if there is someone to bring the van back. You can collect the money for it. I will be satisfied with the trip."

He looked at me in joy. "But yes, it can be arranged, my mate drives, we have to load furniture from a big house here and take it to Caen and unload it." By fast work it was arranged. On the morrow I was going to be a furniture remover's assistant, unpaid.

Henri, the driver, could easily have obtained a certificate of incompetence. In one thing only was he a past-master. He knew every dodge imaginable to get out of doing work. Just out of sight of the house, he stopped and said, "You drive, I'm tired." He wandered round to the back, perched on the most comfortable furnishings he could find, and went to sleep. I drove.

At Caen he said, "You start unloading, I must get these papers signed." Everything except the two-man things were in the house by the time he returned. Slouching off again, he returned with the gardener who helped me carry things in. He "directed" us so that the walls would not be damaged! Unloaded, I climbed into the driver's seat. Henri unthinkingly climbed up beside me. I turned the van and drove to the railway station which I had noticed some way up the road. There I stopped, took out my two cases, and said to Henri, "Now you drive!" With that I turned and entered the station.

There was a train for Cherbourg in twenty minutes. I bought my ticket, had something to eat, and then the train just pulled in. We rattled off into the growing dusk. At Cherbourg Town Station I left my two cases and wandered off down the Quai de 1'Entrepot looking for accommodation At last I found it, Lodgings for Seamen. I entered, booked a very modest room, paid in advance, and went back for my luggage. Being tired, I went to bed and slept.

In the morning I associated as much as possible with other lodger-seamen who were waiting for ships. By great good fortune I was during the next few days able to visit the engine rooms of vessels at the Port. During the week I haunted the Shipping Agents in search of an appointment which would take me across the Atlantic. The Agents would look at my papers, examine my Discharge Book, and ask, "So you ran out of funds on vacation? and want to work a one-way trick? All right, we will keep you in mind and let you know if anything turns up." I mixed more and more with seamen, learning their terminology, learning all that I could of personalities. Above all I learned that the less one said and the more one listened, the greater one's reputation for intelligence became.

At last, after some ten days, I was called to a Shipping Agent's Office. A short, square looking man was sitting with the Agent. "Are you free to sail tonight, if wanted?" asked the Agent.

"I am free to sail now, sir," I replied. The short, square man was watching me closely. Then he shot out a spate of questions in an accent which I found hard to follow. "The Chief here is a Scotsman, his Third Engineer has fallen sick and has been taken to hospital. He wants you to go aboard with him immediately," translated the Agent. By great concentration I was able to follow the rest of the Scotsman's speech and was able to answer his questions satisfactorily. "Get your dunnage," he said at last, "and come aboard."

Back at the Lodging House I hastily settled my bill, picked up my cases, and hired a cab to the ship's side. She was a battered old thing, rust streaked, sadly in need of a coat of paint, and woefully small for Atlantic crossings. "Aye," said a man on the dockside, "she's past her prime ye ken, and in a following sea she wallows fit t' twist yer guts out!"

I hurried up the gangplank, left my cases by the galley, and clattered down the iron ladder to the engine room where Chief Mac was waiting. He discussed the engines with me and was satisfied with my answers. "Okay, Laddie," he said at last, "we'll go an' sign the Articles. The Steward will show you to your cabin." We hastened back to the Shipping Office, "signed Articles", and then returned to the ship. "Ye're on straight away, Laddie," said Mac. So, probably for the first time in history, a Tibetan Lama, posing as an American, took his place aboard ship as a watch-keeping engineer. The eight hours I first served, with the ship moored, was a blessing to me. My intensive reading was now supplemented by some practical experience, and I felt fully confident.

With the clanging of bells, and the noisy hissing of steam, the shining steel rods rose and fell, rose and fell. Wheels turned faster and faster, bringing the ship to life. There was the smell of heated oil and steam. To me this was a strange life, as strange as life in a lamasery would be to Chief Mac who now stood so stolidly, pipe between his teeth, one hand resting lightly on a glittering steel control wheel. The bell clanged again and the telegraph dial indicated "half astern". With scarcely a glance Mac spun the wheel and flicked a lever. The thudding of the engine increased and the whole hull quivered lightly. "Stop!" said the telegraph dial, followed quickly by "half ahead". Almost before Mac could spin the controls, the bell clanged again for "full-ahead". Smoothly the ship forged ahead. Mac stepped forward to me, "Ah, Laddie," he said, "ye've done yer eight hours. Be off with ye. Tell the Steward Ah want ma cocoa as ye step by."

Cocoa, food! It reminded me that I had not eaten for more than twelve hours. Hastily I climbed the steel ladders, reaching the deck and the open air. Spray was breaking over the bows, and the ship plunged somewhat as we headed out into open sea. Behind me the lights of the French coast were fading into the darkness. A sharp voice behind me brought me back to the present: "Who are you, my man?" I turned and saw the First Mate standing beside me.

"Third Engineer, sir," I answered.

"Then why are you not in uniform?"

"I am a relief engineer, sir, joined at Cherbourg and went on watch immediately."

"Hrrumph," said the Mate. "Get into uniform right away, we must have discipline here." With that he stalked off as if he were First Mate on one of the Queens instead of just on a dirty, rusty old tramp ship.

At the galley door I gave Chief Mac's order. "You the new Third?" said a voice behind me. I turned and saw the Second Engineer who had just entered. "Yes, sir," I replied. "I am just on my way to get into uniform and then I want some food."

He nodded, "I will come along with you. The Mate has just complained that you are out of uniform. Said he thought you were a stowaway. Told him you had just joined and had gone straight on duty." He walked along with me and pointed out that my cabin was just across the alley from his. "Call when you are ready," he said, "and we will go for dinner."

I had had to have the uniforms altered to fit me. Now as I stood dressed as a Merchant Marine Officer I wondered what my Guide the Lama Mingyar Dondup would say if he could see me. It made me chuckle to think what a sensation I would be in Lhasa if I appeared there dressed thus. Calling for the Second Engineer, we walked together back to the Officers' Mess for dinner.

84

The Captain, already at his table, gave us a scowling glance from beneath his bushy eyebrows.

"Faugh!" said the Second Engineer, when the first course was placed before him. "Same old pig-swill, don't you ever get a change round here?"

"Mister!" The Captain's voice nearly lifted us from our seats. "Mister! You are always complaining, you should change to another ship when we get to New York."

Somebody started to snigger, a snigger which changed to an embarrassed cough as the Captain looked angrily in his direction. The rest of the meal was in silence until the Captain, finished before us, left. "Hell ship," said one officer. "The Old Man was a Jimmy-the-One (First Mate) in the British Navy during the war. He was on a transport and he cannot get it out of his system."

"Aw, you guys is nuts, always bellyachin'," said another voice.

"No," whispered the Second to me, "he is not American, just a Puerto Rican who has seen too many movies."

I was tired, and went out on deck before turning in. Just off to the lee side the men were dumping the hot ashes in the sea and getting rid of the accumulated garbage of a stay in port. The ship was tossing a bit, and I walked off to my cabin. The walls were plastered with pin-up girls, which I ripped off and tossed into the waste paper basket. As I undressed and tumbled into my bunk I knew that I would be able to carry out my duties.

"Time up!" yelled a voice, and a hand opened the door and flicked on the light switch. "Time already?" I thought to myself. Why, it seemed that I had barely got to sleep. I glanced at my watch, and rolled out. A wash, dressed, and I was on my way to breakfast. The Mess was deserted now, and I ate alone and quickly. With a glance outside at the first streaks of light across the side, I hurried down the steel ladders to the engine room. "You're punctual," said the Second Engineer. "That I like. Nothing to report except that there are two greasers in the tunnel. Oh well, I'm going," he said, yawning heavily.

The engines thudded on rhythmically, monotonously, every revolution bringing us nearer to New York. Outside in the stokehold the "black-gang" tended their fires, raking and slicing, keeping the head of steam just short of the red line. From out of the tunnel housing the propeller shaft two sweat-stained and dirty men emerged. Fortune was with me, bearing temperatures

85

were normal, there was nothing to report. Grubby papers were shoved at me, coal consumed, C percentages, and other data. I signed, sat down, and wrote up the Engine Room Log for my watch. "How she doin' Mister?" said Mac as he came clattering down the companionway.

"All right," I answered. "Everything normal."

"Good," said Mac. "I wish I could make that– Captain normal. He says we used too much coal last trip. What should I do? Tell him to row the ship. He sighed, put on steel-framed glasses, read the Log and signed it.

The ship forged on through the rough Atlantic. Day followed day in monotonous sameness. This was not a happy ship, the Deck Officers sneered at the Engine staff. The Captain was a gloomy man who thought he commanded an Atlantic liner instead of a wallowing old tub of a freighter. Even the weather was bad. One night I could not sleep for the heaving and tossing, and I went on deck. The wind was howling through the rigging in a depressing threnody, reminding me irresistibly of the time when I had stood upon the roof of the Chakpori with the Lama Mingyar Dondup and Jigme, and went off into the astral. At the lee side of the ship, amidships, a lonely figure clutched desperately at the rail and heaved and heaved, almost "bringing his heart up", as he later said. I was quite immune to seasickness, and found considerable amusement at the sight of life-long sailors being bowled over like this. The binnacle light in the bridge cast the faintest glow upwards. In the Captain's cabin all was dark. Spray rushed over the bows and swept aft to where I was standing. The ship rolled and tossed like a thing demented, with the masts describing a crazy arc across the night sky. Far off to starboard an Atlantic liner, all lights blazing, came towards us, corkscrewing with a motion which must have left the passengers unhappy. With a following wind she was making good time, her immense superstructure acting as a sail. "She'll soon be in Southampton Roads," I thought to myself as I turned to go below.

At the height of the storm one of the bilge pump intakes clogged on something dislodged by the violence of the ship's motion, and I had to go right down in the bilge and supervise the men who were working on it. The noise was terrific, the propeller shaft was vibrating as the propeller alternately raced madly when the ship's stern was in the air, and juddered when the stern dipped in the water before bouncing to the crest of the next wave.

In the holds the deckmen were working feverishly securing a heavy crate of machinery which had broken loose. It seemed to me so strange that there was so much friction on this ship, we were all doing our jobs to the best of our

86

abilities. What did it matter if one man worked among machines in the bowels of the ship, while another walked the deck, or stood in the Docking Bridge to watch the water slide along the side of the ship?

Work? There was plenty of work here, pumps to be overhauled, stuffing boxes to be repacked, glands to be inspected and checked, and the lines to the winches overhauled in preparation for docking at New York.

Chief Mac himself was a good worker and a fair man. He loved his engines as a mother loves her first born child. One afternoon I was sitting on a grating waiting to go on watch. Light storm-clouds scudded across the sky, and there was a hint of the heavy rain which was to follow. I sat in the shelter of a ventilator, reading. Suddenly a heavy hand descended upon my shoulder, and a booming Scottish voice said, "Ah! Laddie, I wondered what ye did with yer spare time. What is it? Westerns? Sex ?"

Smilingly I passed the book to him. "Marine engines," I said. "More interesting to me than Westerns—or Sex!"

He grunted approvingly as he glanced through the book before passing it back to me. "Guid fer ye, Laddie," he said. "We'll make an engineer of ye yet, and ye'll soon be a Chief yer'sel if ye stick to that." Pushing his battered old pipe back in his mouth, he nodded amiably to me and said, "Ye can take over now, Laddie."

The ship was abustle. "Captain's Inspection, Third," whispered the Second. "He's a crazy guy, thinks he's on a liner, inspects the whole ship—cabins and all—every trip."

I stood beside my bunk as the Captain entered, followed by the First Mate and the Purser. "Hum," muttered the Great Man as he glanced disdainfully around. "No pin-ups?" he said. "I thought all Americans were leg-crazy!" He glanced at my engineering books, and a cynical smile played round his mouth. "Is there a novel inside that technical cover?" he asked. Without a word I stepped forward and opened every book at random. The Captain rubbed a finger here and there, on a rail, beneath the bunk, and on top of the door ledge. Looking at his still clean fingertips, he nodded in disappointment and stalked out. The Second smiled knowingly, "You got him that time, he's a nosey—!"

There was an air of tense expectancy. Men were getting out their shore-going togs, cleaning themselves up, trying to decide how to get their parcels through Customs. Men were talking of their families, of their girl-friends. All tongues were loosened, all restraints thrown off. Soon they would be ashore to go to friends and loved ones. Only I had nowhere to go, no one of whom to talk. Only I would walk ashore at New York as a stranger, friendless, unknown.

On the skyline stood the tall towers of Manhattan glistening in the sunlight after being washed by the rainstorm. Isolated windows threw back the rays of the sun after turning them to burnished gold. The Statue of Liberty— I noticed with her back to America—loomed up before us. "Half ahead," clanged the telegraph. The ship slowed, and the little bow wave died as our momentum dropped. "Stop," said the telegraph as we nosed to our berth. Lines were thrown, and caught, and the ship was once more tied to the land. "Finished with engines," said the telegraph. Steam died in the pipes with wailing hisses. The giant piston rods were stilled, and the ship wallowed gently at her moorings, but faintly disturbed by the wake of passing ships. We worked turning valves, bringing the auxiliary equipment to life, hoists and winches.

Up on deck men rushed round knocking the wedges off the hatch covers, dragging off tarpaulins, opening the holds. The Ship's Agents came aboard, followed by the stevedores. Soon the ship was a madhouse of raucous voices bellowing commands. The cranes rattled and chuffed, and there was the continuous scuffle of heavy feet. The Port Medical Officer's Deputy pored over the crew records. Police came aboard and took off a wretched stowaway of whom we in the Engine Room had heard nothing. The unfortunate man was led off in handcuffs, escorted by two burly, rough- looking policemen who led him to a waiting Police car and urgently pushed him inside.

We lined up, collected our money, signed for it and went on to get our Discharge Books. Chief Mac had written in mine, "Great devotion to duty. Efficient in all branches. Shall welcome him as a shipmate at any time." "What a pity," I thought, "that I have to scrap all this, that I cannot continue."

I went back to my cabin and tidied up, folding the blankets and putting them aside. Packing my books, dressing in civilian clothes, and placing my gear in the two suitcases. With a last look round I went out and shut the door behind me.

"Will ye no' change yer mind?" said Chief Mac. "Yer a guid shipmate, and I'd be glad t' put ye in fer Second after this round trip."

"No, Chief," I answered, "I want to move around a bit and get more experience."

"Experience is a wunnerful thing. Guid luck t' ye!"

I walked down the gangplank carrying my two cases. Off by the side of the moored ships. Another life before me; how I hated all this moving round, all this uncertainty, with no one to call "friend".

"Where ya born?" said the Customs man.

"Pasadena," I replied, thinking of the papers in my hand.

"What ya got?" he demanded.

"Nothing," I told him. He looked at me sharply, "Okay, open up," he snarled. Placing my cases before him I opened them. He rummaged and rummaged, then tipped everything out and examined the linings. "Pack 'em up," he said as he walked away and left me.

I packed my cases again, and walked out of the gates. Outside, in the mad roar of traffic, I stopped a moment to get my bearings and my breath. "Wassamadderwidyabud ? Disisnooyoik!" said a crude voice behind me. Turning, I saw a policeman glaring at me.

"Any crime in stopping?" I answered him.

"Awgitmovin!" he bellowed.

Slowly I picked up my suitcases and wandered up the road, marveling at the man-made metal mountains of Manhattan, I had never felt lonelier than now, completely alien to this part of the world. Behind me the roaring cop bellowed at some other unfortunate, "Wedontdodisinnooyoik. Git!" The people looked harassed, strained. Motor vehicles zoomed by at crazy speeds. There was the continual squeal of tyres and the smell of burning rubber.

I walked on. At last I saw before me the sign "Seamen's Hostel," and I gratefully turned in at the door. "Sign," said a cold, impersonal voice. Carefully I completed the form thrust roughly at me, and handed it back with a "thank you". "Don't thank me," said the cold voice, "I am not doing you any favor, this is my job." I stood waiting. "Well, what is it?" said the voice. "Room three-oh-three, it said so on the form and on the key tag."

I turned away. How could one argue with a human automaton. I walked over to a man, obviously a sailor, sitting in a chair looking at a man's magazine. "We guys sure get in Jenny's hair," he said before I could speak. "What is your room number?"

89

"Three-oh-three," I answered miserably. "My first time here."

"Three floors up," he said. "It'll be the third room to starboard." Thanking him, I walked over to a door marked "Elevator." "Go and press the button," said the man in the chair. I did so, and after some moments the door was flung open, and a Negro boy beckoned me in. "Number?" he asked.

"Three-oh-three," I replied. He pressed a button and the little room moved swiftly up and came to a sudden halt. The Negro boy opened the door and said, "Toid." The door closed behind me, and I was alone once more.

Fumblingly, I looked at the key tag to again check the number, and then moved along to find my room. Yes— there it was—the number "303" was on a small plate above the third door to the right of the elevator. I inserted the key and turned it. The door opened, and I entered the room. Quite a small room, I saw, something like a ship's cabin. As soon as I shut the door I saw a printed list of Rules. Carefully reading them, I found that I could stay only twenty-four hours unless I was actually joining a ship, then the maximum time one was permitted to stay was forty-eight hours. Twenty four hours! So even now there was no peace. I set down my cases, brushed the dust from me, and went out in search of food and newspapers so that I could see if there were any jobs advertised which I could do.

Chapter Six

New York seemed such an unfriendly place. People whom I attempted to stop to enquire the way gave me a frightened look and hurried on. After a night's sleep, I had my breakfast and boarded a bus for the Bronx. From the papers I had gained the idea that lodgings would be cheaper there. Near Bronx Park I alighted and trudged along the street looking for a "Room for Rent" sign. A speeding car flashed between two delivery vans and on to the wrong side of the road, skidding, it mounted the sidewalk and struck me on the left side. Once again I heard the breaking of bones. As I slid to the sidewalk, and before merciful oblivion claimed me, I saw a man snatch up my two suitcases and hurry off.

The air was filled of the sound of music. I was happy, comfortable after years of hardship. "Ah!" exclaimed the voice of the Lama Mingyar Dondup, "So you have had to come here again?" I opened my eyes to find him smiling down upon me, with the utmost compassion shining from his eyes. "Life upon Earth is hard and bitter, and you have had experiences from which, happily, most people are spared. It is just an interlude, Lobsang, just an unpleasant interlude. After the long night will come the awakening to a perfect day when no longer need you return to Earth, nor to any of the lower worlds." I sighed. It was pleasant here, and that accentuated even more the harshness and unfairness of the Earth life. "You, my Lobsang," said my Guide, "are living your last, life upon Earth. You are clearing up all Kharma and are also doing a momentous task, a task which evil powers seek to hinder."

Kharma! It recalled vividly to my mind the lesson, which I had learned in beloved, far-off Lhasa....

The tinkling of the little silver bells had ended. No longer did the trumpets blare across the Valley of Lhasa, sounding loud and clear in the crisp, thin air. About me was uncanny silence, a silence that should not be. I awakened from my reverie just as the monks in the temple started their deep-toned Litany for the Dead. Dead? Yes! Of course, the Litany for the old monk who had so recently died. Died, after a life-time of suffering, of service to others, of being misunderstood and unthanked.

"What a terrible Kharma he must have had," I said to myself "What a wicked person he must have been in his past life to merit such retribution."

"Lobsang!" The voice behind me was like a clap of distant thunder. The blows that rained upon my shrinking body—well—they were not so distant, unfortunately. "Lobsang! You here skulking, showing disrespect to our departed Brother, take that, and that!" Suddenly the blows and the abuse stopped as if by magic. I turned my anguished head round and gazed up at the giant figure towering above me, heavy cudgel still in his upraised hand.

"Proctor," said a well-loved voice, "that was vicious punishment indeed for a small boy. What has he done to suffer that? Has he desecrated the Temple? Has he shown disrespect to the Golden Figures? Speak, and explain your cruelty."

"Lord Mingyar Dondup," whined the tall Proctor of the Temple, "the boy was here day-dreaming when he should have been at the Litany with his fellows."

The Lama Mingyar Dondup, no small man himself, gazed sadly up at the seven-foot Man of Kham standing before him. Firmly the Lama spoke, "You may go, Proctor, I will deal with this myself". As the Proctor respectfully bowed, and turned away, my Guide, the Lama Mingyar Dondup turned to me, "Now Lobsang, let us go to my room so that you can recount the tale of your numerous well punished sins." With that he stooped gently and lifted me to my feet. In my short life no one but my Guide had ever shown me kindness, and I was hard put to keep back tears of gratitude and love.

The Lama turned away and slowly walked up the long deserted corridor. I humbly followed in his footsteps, followed even eagerly, knowing that no injustice could ever come from this great man.

At the entrance to his room he stopped, turned to me, and put a hand on my shoulder, "Come along, Lobsang, you have committed no crime, come in and tell me about this trouble." With that he pushed me before him and bade me be seated. "Food, Lobsang, "Food", that also is upon your mind. We must have food and tea while we talk." Leisurely he rang his silver bell, and an attendant entered.

Until food and drink was placed before us we sat in silence, I thinking of the sureness with which all my offences were found out and punished almost before they were committed. Once again a voice broke into my thoughts. "Lobsang! You are day-dreaming! Food, Lobsang, Food is before you and you, you of all people, do not see it." The kindly, bantering voice brought me back to attention and almost automatically I reached out for those sweet sugared cakes which so greatly entranced my palate. Cakes which had been

92

brought from far-off India for the Dalai Lama, but which through his kindness were available to me.

For some moments more we sat and ate, or rather I ate, and the Lama smiled benevolently upon me. "Now, Lobsang," he said when I showed signs of repletion, "what is all this about?"

"Master," I replied, "I was reflecting upon the terrible Kharma of the monk who died. He must have been a very wicked man in many lives past. So thinking, I forgot all about the temple service, and the Proctor came upon me before I was able to escape."

He burst out with a laugh, "So, Lobsang, you would have tried to escape from your Kharma if you could!" I looked glumly at him, knowing that few could outrun the athletic proctors, so very fleet of foot.

"Lobsang, this matter of Kharma. Oh how it is misunderstood by some even here in the Temple. Make yourself comfortable, for I am going to talk to you on this matter at some length."

I shuffled around a bit and made a show of "getting comfortable". I wanted to be out with the others, not sitting here listening to a lecture, for even from such a great man as the Lama Mingyar Dondup a lecture was a lecture, and medicine with a pleasant taste was still medicine.

"You know all this, Lobsang, or should if you have paid any attention to your teachers (which I doubt!) but I will remind you again as I fear that your attention is still somewhat lacking." With that he gave me a piercing glance and resumed. "We come to this Earth as to a school. We come to learn our lessons. In our first attendance at school we are in the lowest class because we are ignorant and as yet have learned nothing. At the end of our term we either pass our examinations or fail them. If we pass we go on to a higher class, when we return from the school vacation. If we fail, then we return to the same class as that which we left. If we fail in perhaps one subject only we may be permitted to go on to the higher class and there also study the subject of our failure."

This was speaking to me in language, which I well understood. I knew all about examinations, and failing in a subject and having to go on to a higher class, competing with bigger boys, and at the same time studying in what should have been my free time, studying under the eagle eye of some mouldy old lama teacher, one who was so ancient that he forgot all about his own boyhood days.

93

There was a crash, and I jumped so much with fright that I almost left the ground. "Ah, Lobsang, so we did get a reaction after all," said my Guide as he laughingly replaced the silver bell he had dropped behind me; "I spoke to you on a number of occasions, but you were wandering far afield."

"I am sorry, Honourable Lama," I replied, "but I was thinking how clear your lecture was."

The Lama stilled a smile and continued. "We come to this Earth as do children to a schoolroom. If, in our lifetime, we do well and learn that which caused us to come, then we progress further and take up life in a higher state. If we do not learn our lessons, we come back to almost the same type of body and conditions. In some cases a man, in a past life, will have shown much cruelty to others. He must come back to this Earth and try to atone for his misdeeds. He must come back and show kindness to others.

Many of the greatest reformers in this life were offenders in the past. So the Wheel of Life revolves, bringing first riches to one, and then poverty to another, and the beggar of today may be the prince of tomorrow, and so it continues from life to life."

"But Honourable Lama," I interjected, "does it mean that if a man is now a beggar with one leg, he must have cut off the leg of some other person in another life?"

"No, Lobsang, it does not. It means that the man needed to be poor, and needed to suffer the loss of one leg so that he could learn his lesson. If you have to study figures you take your slate and your abacus. If you are going to study carving you take a knife and a piece of wood. You take tools suitable for the task in hand. So it is with the type of body we have, the body and our life circumstances are the most suitable for the task we have to overcome."

I thought of the old monk who had died, he was always bewailing his "bad Kharma", wondering what he had done to deserve such a hard life. "Ah, yes, Lobsang," said my Guide, reading my thoughts, "the unenlightened always bemoan the workings of Kharma. They do not realize that they are sometimes the victims of the bad acts of others, and though they suffer unjustly now, yet in a later life they will have full recompense. Again I say to you, Lobsang, you cannot judge a man's evolution by his present status on Earth, nor can you condemn him as evil because he seems to be in difficulties. Nor should you condemn, for until you have all the facts, which you cannot have in this life, you have no sound judgment."

94

The voice of the temple trumpets echoing through the halls and corridors summoned us from our talk to attend the evening service. Voice of the temple trumpets? Or was it a deep-toned gong? It seemed that the gong was in my head, booming away, jerking me, bringing me back to life on Earth. Wearily I opened my eyes. Screens were around my bed and an oxygen cylinder stood nearby. "He is awake, Doctor," said a voice. Shuffling of feet, and the rustle of well-starched cloth. A red face came into range of my vision. "Ah!" said the American doctor. "So you have come back to life! You sure got yourself smashed up!" I gazed blankly at him.

"My suitcases?" I asked, "Are they all right?"

"No, a guy made off with them and the police cannot find him."

Later in the day the police came to my bedside seeking information. My cases had been stolen. The man whose car had knocked me down and gravely injured me was not insured. He was an unemployed negro. Once again I had my left arm broken, four ribs broken, and both feet smashed. "You will be out in a month," cheerily said the doctor. Then double pneumonia set in. For nine weeks I lingered in the hospital. As soon as I was able to get up I was asked about payment. "We found two hundred and sixty dollars in your wallet, we shall have to take two hundred and fifty for your stay here." I looked at the man aghast. "But I shall have no job, nothing," I said. "How shall I live on ten dollars?"

The man shrugged his shoulders. "Oh you will have to sue the negro. You have had treatment and we have to be paid. The case is nothing to do with us—make an action against the man who caused the trouble."

Shakily I went down the stairs. Tottered into the street. No money, other than ten dollars. No job, nowhere to live. How to live, that was the problem. The janitor jerked his thumb, "Up the street, Employment Agency there, go see them." Nodding dumbly, I wandered off, looking for my only hope. In a shoddy side-street I saw a battered sign, "Jobs". The climb to the third floor office was almost more than I could manage. Gasping, I clung to the rail at the top until I felt a little better.

"Kin ye scrub, Bud?" said the yellow-toothed man, rolling a ragged cigar between his thick lips. He eyed me up and down. "Guess you have just come out of the penitentiary or the hospital," he said. I told him all that had happened, how I had lost my belongings and my money. "So you want some bucks mighty fast," he said, reaching for a card and filling in some details. He gave it to me, and told me to take it to a hotel with a very celebrated name, one of the hotels! I went, spending precious cents on bus fares.

95

"Twenty dollars a week and one meal per day," said the Staff Manager. So, for "twenty dollars and one meal per day" I washed mountains of filthy plates, and scrubbed endless stairs for ten hours each day.

Twenty dollars a week—and one meal. The meals served to the staff were not of the same quality as those served to the guests. Staff meals were rigidly supervised and checked. My wages were so poor that I could not afford a room. I made my home in the parks, beneath arches and bridges, and learned to move at night before the Cop on the Beat came along with his prodding night stick and his gruff "Getamoveonwillya?" I learned to stuff my clothes with newspaper to keep out the bitter winds that swept New York's deserted streets by night. My one suit of clothes was travel-worn and work-stained, and I had no change of underwear. To wash my clothing I locked myself in the Men's Room, removed my underwear, put my trousers on again, and washed my clothing in a basin, drying them on the steam pipes after, for until I could wear them I could not go out. My shoes had holes in the soles, and I patched them with cardboard, while watching the garbage bins for any better pair which a guest might throw out. But there were many keen eyes and many eager hands to examine the "guest-trash" before it reached me. I lived and worked on one meal a day, and plenty of water. Gradually I accumulated a change of clothing, a second-hand suit, and second-hand shoes. Slowly I accumulated a hundred dollars.

One day I heard two guests talking as I worked near a service door. They were discussing the failure of an advertisement to bring in a reply from the type of man they wanted. I worked slower and slower. "Knowledge of Europe. Good voice, radio training..." Something happened to me, I dashed round the door and exclaimed, "I can claim all those!" The men looked at me dumbfounded and then broke into yells of laughter. The Chief Waiter and an under waiter dashed forward, utter fury on their faces. "Out!" said the Chief Waiter as he grabbed violently at my collar, ripping my poor old jacket from top to bottom. I turned on him and threw the two halves of my jacket in his face: "Twenty dollars a week does not enable you to speak to a man like that!" I said fiercely. One of the two men looked at me in hushed horror, "Twenty dollars a week, you said?"

"Yes, sir, that is what I am paid, and one meal a day. I sleep in the parks, I am chased from place to place by the police. I came to this 'Land of Opportunity' and on the day after I landed a man ran me down with his car, and when I was unconscious an American robbed me of all I had. Proof? Sir? I will give you proof, then you check my story!" The Floor Manager rushed up, wringing his hands and almost weeping. We were ushered into his office. The others sat down, I was left standing. The older of the two men phoned the

96

hospital, and after some delay, my story was authenticated in every detail. The Floor Manager pressed a twenty-dollar bill on me, "Buy a new jacket," he said, "and clear out!" I pressed the money back into his flabby hands. "You take it," I replied, "You will need it more than I." I turned to leave and as I reached the door a hand shot out and a voice said "Stop!" The older man looked me straight in the eyes. "I think that you may suit us. We will see. Come to Schenectady tomorrow. Here is my card." I turned to go. "Wait— here are fifty dollars to see you there."

"Sir," I said, refusing the money offered, "I will get there under my own steam. I will not take money until you are sure that I will meet your requirements, for I could not possibly pay you back if you do not want me." I turned and left the room. From my locker in the Staff Room I took my meagre belongings and walked out in the street. I had nowhere to go but to a seat in the park. No roof, no one to whom to say good-bye. In the night the pitiless rain came down and soaked me to the skin. By good fortune I kept my "new suit" dry by sitting on it.

In the morning I had a cup of coffee and a sandwich and found that the cheapest way to travel from New York City to Schenectady was by bus. I bought my ticket and settled in a seat. Some passenger had left a copy of the Morning Times on a seat, so I read through it to keep me from brooding on my very uncertain future. The bus droned on, eating up the miles. By afternoon I was in the city. I went to the public baths, made myself as smart as possible, put on my clean clothes and walked out.

At the radio studios the two men were waiting. For hour after hour they plied me with questions. Man after man came in and went out again. At last they had my whole story. "You say you have papers stored with a friend in Shanghai?" said the senior man. "Then we will engage you on a temporary basis and will cable to Shanghai to have your things sent on here. As soon as we see these papers, you will be on a permanent footing. A hundred and ten dollars a week; we will discuss it further when we see those papers. Have them sent at our expense."

The second man spoke, "Sure guess he could do with an advance," he said.

"Give him a month in advance," said the first man. "Let him start the day after tomorrow."

So began a happy period in my life. I liked the work, and I gave complete satisfaction. In the course of time my papers, my age-old crystal, and a very few other things arrived. The two men checked everything, and gave me a fifteen dollar a week raise. Life was beginning to smile upon me, I thought.

After some time, during which I saved most of my money, I began to experience the feeling that I was getting nowhere, I was not getting on with my allotted task in life. The senior man was very fond of me now, and I went to him and discussed the problem, telling him that I would leave when he found a suitable replacement for me. For three months more I stayed.

My papers had come from Shanghai, among them a passport issued by the British authorities at the British Concession. During those far-off war days the British were very fond of me, for they made use of my services. Now, well, now they think they have no more to gain. I took my passport and other papers to the United Kingdom Embassy in New York, and after a lot of trouble and much delay, managed to obtain first a visa and then a work permit for England.

At last a replacement for me was obtained, and I stayed two weeks to "show him the ropes", then I left. America is perhaps unique in that a person who knows how, can travel almost anywhere free. I looked at various newspapers until I saw, under "Transportation", the following:

"California, Seattle, Boston, New York.

Gas free, Call 000000 XXX Auto Drive-away."

Firms in America want cars delivered all over the continent. Many drivers want to travel, so a good and cheap method is for the would-be driver to get in touch with the auto delivery firm. On passing a simple driving test one is then given gas (petrol) vouchers for certain selected filling stations on the route.

I called on the XXX Auto Drive-away and said I wanted to drive a car to Seattle. "No difficulty at all, at all," said the man with the Irish brogue. "I am looking for a good driver to take a Lincoln there. Drive me round, let's see how you shape." As I drove him round he told me of various useful matters. He seemed to have taken quite a liking to me, then he said; "I recognized your voice, you were an Announcer." This I confirmed. He said, "I have a short-wave radio which I use to keep in touch with the Old Country. Something wrong with it, it won't get the short waves any more. The local men do not understand this type of radio, do you?"

I assured him that I would have a look at it and he invited me to his home

98

that evening, even lending me a car with which to get there. His Irish wife was exceptionally pleasant, and they left within me a love for Ireland, which became intensified when I went there to live.

The radio was a very famous English model, an exceptionally fine Eddystone which has no peer. Fortune smiled upon me. The Irishman picked up one of the plug-in coils and I saw how he held it. "Let me have that coil," I said, "and have you a magnifying glass?" He had, and a quick examination showed me that in his incorrect handling of the coil, he had broken a wire free from one of the pins. I showed it to him. "Have you a soldering iron and solder?" I asked. No, but his neighbour had. Off he dashed, to return with a soldering iron and solder. It was the work of minutes to resolder the wire—and the set worked. Simple little adjustments to the trimmers and it worked better. Soon we were listening to the B.B.C. in London, England.

"I was going to send the radio back to England to be put right," said the Irishman. "Now I'm going to do something for you. The owner of the Lincoln wanted one of our firm's drivers to take it to him in Seattle. He is a rich man. I am going to put you on our payroll so you can get paid. We will give you eighty dollars and we will charge him a hundred and twenty. Done?" Done? Most certainly, it suited me just fine.

On the following Monday morning I started off. Pasadena. was my first destination. I wanted to make sure that the Ship's Engineer whose papers I had used really had no relatives. New York, Pittsburg, Columbus, Kansas City, the miles mounted up. I did not hurry, I allowed a week for the trip. By night I slept in the big car to save hotel expenses, pulling off the road wherever I thought suitable. Soon I was at the foot-hills of the American Rockies, enjoying the better air, enjoying it even more as the car climbed higher and higher. For a whole day I lingered here in the mountainous ranges, and then I drove off to Pasadena. The most scrupulous enquiries failed to reveal that the Engineer had any relatives. He seemed to have been a morose sort of man who preferred his own company to that of any other person.

Through the Yosemite National Park I drove. Crater Lake National Park, Portland, and finally Seattle. I took the car into the garage where it was carefully inspected, greased and washed. Then a call was made by the garage manager. "Come on," he said to me, "he wants us to take it over to him." I drove the Lincoln, and the manager drove another car so that we had return transportation.

Up the spacious drive of a big house, and three men appeared. The manager was very deferential to the frosty-faced man who had bought the Lincoln.

The two men with him were automobile engineers who proceeded to give the Lincoln a thorough examination. "It has been very carefully driven," said the senior engineer, "you may take delivery with complete confidence."

The frosty-faced man nodded condescendingly at me. "Come along to my study," he said, "I am going to give you a bonus of a hundred dollars—for you alone—because you have driven so carefully."

"Man, oh! Man!" said the manager afterwards. "That was mighty big of him, you sure made a hit."

"I want a job taking me into Canada," I said. "Can you help me?"

"Well," replied the manager, "you really want to go to Vancouver and I have nothing in that direction, but I have a man who wants a new De Soto. He lives at Oroville, right on the Border. He will not drive that far himself. He'd be mighty glad to have someone deliver his car. His credit is good. I'll call him."

"Gee, Hank!" said the manager to the man on the telephone, "Will ye quit yer dickering! and say if you want the De Soto?" He listened for a while and then broke in, "Well, ain't I a-telling you? I gotta guy here who is coming to Oroville on his way to Canada. He brought a Lincoln from New York. What say, Hank?" Hank babbled away at length in Oroville. His voice came through to me as a confused jumble of sound. The manager sighed with exasperation. "Well, ain't you an ornery doggone crittur?" he said. "You can place your cheque in the bank, guess I've known you for twenty years and more, not scairt of you running out on me." He listened for a little longer. "OO-kay," he said at last, "I will do that. Yep, I'll add it on the bill." He hung up the receiver and let out his breath in a long, low whistle. "Say, Mister," he said to me, "D'ye know anything about wimmen?" Women? What did he think I knew about women? Who does know about them? They are enigmas even to themselves! The manager saw my blank look and continued, "Hank up there, he's been a bachelor for forty years, that I know. Now he asks for you to bring up some feminine fripperies for him. Well, well, well, guess the ol' daug's gone gay. I shall ask the Missus what to send."

Later in the week I drove out to Seattle in a brand new De Soto and a load of women's clothes. Mrs. Manager had sensibly telephoned Hank to see what it was all about! Seattle to Wenatchee, Wenatchee to Oroville. Hank was satisfied, so I wasted little time but pressed on into Canada. For a few days I stayed at Osoyoos. By not a little good fortune I was able to make my way across Canada, from Trail, through Ottawa, Montreal, and Quebec. There is no point in going into that here, because it was so unusual that it may yet be the subject of another book.

Quebec is a beautiful city with the disadvantage that in some parts of it one is unpopular unless one can speak French. My own knowledge of the language was just sufficient to get me through! I frequented the waterfront, and by managing to obtain a Seaman's Union Card, I joined a ship as deck hand. Not a highly paid job, but one which enabled me to work my way across the Atlantic once more. The ship was a dirty old tramp. The Captain and the Mates had long ago lost any enthusiasm for the sea and their ship. Little cleaning work was done. I was unpopular because I did not gamble or talk of affairs with women. I was feared because the attempts of the ship's bully to assert his superiority over me resulted in him screaming for mercy. Two of his gang fared even worse, and I was hauled before the Captain and reprimanded for disabling members of the crew. There was no thought that I was merely defending myself! Apart from those very minor incidents, the journey was uneventful, and soon the ship was making her slow way up the English Channel.

I was off duty and on deck as we passed The Needles and entered the Solent, that strip of water bounded by the Isle of Wight and the mainland. Slowly we crept up past Netley Hospital, with its very beautiful grounds. Up past the busy ferries at Woolston, and into the Harbour at Southampton. The anchor dropped with a splash, and the chain rattled through the hawse-holes. The ship swung head to stream, the engine room telegraph rang out, and the slight vibration of the engine ceased. Officials came aboard, examined the ship's papers and poked about in the crew's quarters. The Port Medical Officer gave us clearance, and slowly the ship steamed up to her moorings. As a member of the crew, I stayed aboard until the ship was unloaded, then, paid off, I took my scanty belongings and went ashore.

"Anything to declare?" asked the Customs Officer.

"Nothing at all," I replied, opening my case as directed. He looked through my few possessions, closed the case, and scribbled his sign on it in chalk.

"How long are you staying?" he asked.

"Going to live here, sir," I replied.

He looked at my Passport, Visa and Work Permit with approval. "Okay," he motioned me through the gate. I walked on, and turned to take a last look at the ship I had just left. A stunning blow almost knocked me to the ground and I turned quickly. Another Customs Officer had been hurrying in from the street, late for duty, he had collided with me and now he sat half dazed in the roadway. For a moment he sat there, then I went to help him up. He struck out at me in fury, so I picked up my case to move on. "Stop!" he yelled.

"It is all right, sir," said the Officer who had passed me through, "He has nothing and his papers are in order."

"I will examine him myself," shouted the Senior Official. Two other Officers stood by me, their faces showing considerable concern. One attempted to remonstrate, but was told roughly to "shut up".

I was taken to a room, and soon the irate Officer appeared. He looked through my case, throwing my things on the floor. He searched the linings and bottom of the battered old case. Chagrined that nothing was to be found, he demanded my Passport. "Ah!" he exclaimed, "You have a Visa and a Work Permit. The Officer in New York had no authority to issue both. It is left to our discretion here in England." He was beaming with triumph, and with a theatrical gesture he tore my Passport right across and threw it in the rubbish container. On an impulse, he picked up the tattered remnants, and stuffed them in his pocket. Ringing a bell, two men came in from the outer office. "This man has no papers," he said, "He will have to be deported, take him to the Holding Cell."

"But, sir" said one of the Officers, "I actually saw them, they were in order."

"Are you questioning my ability?" roared the Senior man. "Do as I say"

A man sadly took my arm. "Come on," he said I was marched out and lodged in a bare cell.

"By Jove, Old Boy!" said the Bright Young Man from the Foreign Office when he entered my cell much, much later. "All this is a frightful pother, what?" He stroked his baby-smooth chin and sighed noisily. "You see our position, Old Chap, it really is just too too simply desperate! You must have had papers, or the Wallahs in Quebec would not have let you embark. Now you have no papers. They must have been lost overboard. Q.E.D. Old Boy, what? I mean to say..."

I glowered at him and remarked, "My papers were deliberately torn up. I demand that I be released and be permitted to land."

"Yes, yes," replied the Bright Young Man, "but can you prove it? I have had a

102

gentle breeze in my ear which told me exactly what happened. We have to stand by our uniformed staff, or the Press would be around our ears. Loyalty and esprit de corps, and all that sort of thing."

"So," I said, "you know the truth, that my papers were destroyed, yet you, in this much-vaunted 'Land of the Free', can stand blandly aside and watch such persecution?"

"My dear fellow, you merely had the Passport of a resident of an Annexed State, you are not a Commonwealth member by birth. I'm afraid you are rather out of our orbit. Now, Chappie, unless you agree that your papers were—ah—lost overboard, we shall have to make a case against you for illegal entry. That might net you a stretch in the cooler for up to two years. If you play ball with us, you will merely be returned to New York."

"New York? Why New York?" I asked.

"If you return to Quebec, you might cause us some trouble. We can prove that you came from New York. So it is up to you. New York or up to two years as an involuntary Guest of His Majesty." He added as an afterthought "Of course, you would still be deported after you had served your sentence, and the Authorities would gladly confiscate that money which you have. Our suggestion will enable you to keep it."

The Bright Young Man stood up and brushed imaginary specks of dust from his immaculate jacket. "Think it over, Old Boy, think it over, we offer you a perfectly wizard way out!" With that he turned and left me alone in the cell.

Stodgy English food was brought in and I attempted to cut it up with the bluntest knife I have ever used. They might have thought that in my extremity I contemplated suicide. Well, no one would commit suicide with that knife.

The day wore on. A friendly Guard tossed in some English newspapers. After a glance I put them aside, so far as I could see they dealt only in sex and scandal. With the coming of darkness I was brought a thick mug of cocoa and a slice of bread and margarine. The night was chilly, with a dankness that reminded me of tombs and mouldering bodies.

The morning Guard greeted me with a smile, which threatened to crack his stony face. "You leave tomorrow," he said. "A ship's Captain has agreed to take you if you work your passage. You will be turned over to the New York Police when you arrive."

Later in the morning an official arrived to tell me officially, and to tell me that I would be doing the hardest work aboard ship, trimming coal in the bunkers of an ancient freighter with no labour saving devices at all. There would be no pay and I would have to sign the Articles to say that I agreed to those terms. In the afternoon I was taken down to the Shipping Agent, under gnard, where—in the presence of the Captain, I signed the Articles.

Twenty-four hours later, still under guard, I was taken to the ship and locked in a small cabin, being told that I would have to remain there until the ship was beyond the limits of territorial waters. Soon the thudding of the old engine awakened the ship to sluggish life. There was the clatter of heavy feet above me and by the rise and fall of the deck I knew that we were heading out into a choppy sea. Not until Portland Bill was well off to starboard, and receding in the distance, was I released. "Git crackin', chum," said the fireman, handing me a battered shovel and rake. "Clean out them there 'oles of clinker. Take 'em on deck and dump 'em. Look lively, now!"

"Aw! Looky here!" bawled the huge man in the fo'c'sle later when I went there. "We gotta Gook, or Chink or Jap. Hey you," he said, slapping me across the face, "Remember Pearl 'Arber?"

"Let 'im be, Butch," said another man, "the cops are arter 'im."

"Haw haw!" roared Butch, "Let's give 'im a workin' over fust, just fer Pearl 'Arber." He sailed in to me, fists going like pistons, and becoming more and more furious as none of his blows reached me. "Slippery swab, eh?" he grunted, reaching out in an attempt to get my throat in a strangle-hold. Old Tzu, and others in far-off Tibet had well prepared me for such things. I dropped, limp, and Butch's momentum carried him forward. He tripped over me and smashed his face on the edge of the fo'c'sle table, breaking his jaw and nearly severing an ear on a mug which he broke in his fall. I had no more trouble with the crew.

Slowly the New York skyline loomed up ahead of us. We ploughed on, leaving a black wake of smoke in the sky from the inferior coal we were using. A Lascar stoker, looking fearfully over his shoulder, edged up to me. "De cops come for you soon," he said. "You good man, heard Chief saying what Cap'n told him. They got to keep their noses clean." He passed me over an oilskin tobacco pouch. "Put your money in that and slip over de side before dey gets you ashore." He whispered confidentially, telling me where the Police boat would head, telling me where I could hide, as he had done in the past. I listened with great care as he told me how to escape the Police hunt after I had jumped overboard. He gave me names and addresses of people who would help me and he promised to get in touch with them when he went ashore. "I have been in trouble like this," he said. "I got framed because of th' colour of ma skin."

"Hey, you!" A voice bawled from the Bridge. "The Cap'n wants you. Double to it!" I hurried up to the Bridge, the Mate jerked a thumb in the direction of the Chart Room. The Captain was sitting at a table, looking over some papers. "Ah!" he said, as he looked up at me. "I have put you in charge of the Police. Have you anything to tell me first?"

"Sir," I replied, "my papers were all in order, but a senior Customs Officer tore them up."

He gazed at me and nodded, looked at his papers again, and apparently made up his mind. "I know the man you mean. I have had trouble with him myself. The face of officialdom must be saved, no matter what misery it causes for others. I know your story is true, for I have a friend at Customs who confirmed your tale." He looked down again and fiddled with the papers "I have a complaint here that you were a stowaway."

"But, sir!" I exclaimed, "the British Embassy in New York can confirm who I am. The Shipping Agents in Quebec can do likewise."

"My man," sadly said the Captain, "You do not know the ways of the West. No enquiries will be made. You will be taken ashore, placed in a cell, tried, convicted, and sent to prison. Then you will be forgotten. When the time for your release is near, you will be detained until you can be deported back to China."

"That will be death, Sir," I said.

He nodded. "Yes, but the course of official duty will have been followed. We on this ship had an experience 'way back in Prohibition days. We were arrested on suspicion and heavily fined, yet we were quite innocent."

He opened the drawer in front of him and took out a small object. "I will tell the Police that you have been framed, I will help you all I can. They may handcuff you, but they will not search you until they get you ashore. Here is a key which fits the Police handcuffs. I will not give it to you, but will place it here, and turn away." He placed the shiny key in front of me, rose from his desk, and turned to the chart behind him. I picked up the key and put it in my pocket.

"Thank you, Sir," I said, "I feel better for your faith in me."

In the distance I saw the Police boat coming up towards us, a white cascade of spray at the bows. Smartly it came alongside, executed a half-turn, and edged in towards us. The ladder was lowered, and two policemen came aboard and made their way up to the Bridge, amid sour looks from members of the crew. The Captain greeted them, giving them a drink and cigars. Then he produced the papers from his desk. "This man has worked well, in my opinion he has been framed by a Government official. Given time to call at the British Embassy, he could prove his innocence."

The senior policeman looked cynical, "All these guys are innocent; the penitentiaries are full of innocent men who have been framed, to listen to them. All we want is to get him tucked nicely in a cell and then we go off duty.

C'mon, fella!" he said to me. I turned to pick up my case. "Aw, you won't want that," he said, hustling me along. On an afterthought he snapped the handcuffs round my wrists.

"Oh, you don't want that," called the Captain. "He can't run anywhere, and how will he get down to your boat?"

"He can fall in the drink and we will fish him out," replied the policeman, laughing coarsely.

Climbing down the ladder was not easy, but I managed it without mishap, to the obvious regret of the police. Once on the cutter, they took no more notice of me. We sped along past many ships and rapidly approached the Police jetty. "Now is the time," I thought, and with a quick leap I was over the side, allowing myself to sink. With acute difficulty I slipped the key in the lock, and turned. The handcuffs came off and sank. Slowly, very slowly, I rose to the surface. The police cutter was a long way off, the men spotted me, and started firing. Bullet splashes were all around me as I sank again. Swimming strongly until I felt that my lungs would burst, I surfaced again. The police were far off, searching round the "obvious place", where I would be expected to land. I crawled ashore at the least obvious place, but will not mention it in case some other unfortunate should need refuge.

For hours I lay on half-sunken timbers, shivering and aching, with the scummy water swirling round me. There came the creak of rowlocks and the splashing of oars in the water. A row boat with three policemen came into sight. I slid off the beam, and let myself sink in the water so that only my nostrils were above the surface. Although I was hidden by the beam, I kept in readiness for instant flight. The boat prowled up and down. At long, long last a hoarse voice said, "Guess he's a stiff by now. His body will be recovered later. Let's get off for some cawfee." The boat drifted out of my range. After a long interval I dragged my aching body on the beam again, shivering almost uncontrollably.

The day ended, and stealthily I inched along the beam to a halfrotten ladder. Gingerly I climbed up, and seeing no one, darted for the shelter of a shed. Stripping off my clothing, I wrung them as dry as possible. Off to the end of the wharf a man appeared, the Lascar. As he came down and was opposite me, I gave a low whistle. He stopped, and sat upon a bollard. "You kin come out cautious-like," he said. "De cops be sure out in force on de udder side. Man! You sure got dem boys rattled." He stood up and stretched, and looked around him. "Follow me," he said, "but I don't know you if you is caught. A coloured gennulmun is waiting wit a truck. When we get dere you climb in de back and cover yo-self with de tarp."

He moved away, and giving him plenty of time, I followed, slipping from one shadowed building to another. The lapping of water around the piles and the far-off wail of a police car were the only sounds disturbing the peace. Suddenly there was the rattle of a truck engine being started and tail lights appeared just ahead. A huge negro nodded to the Lascar and gave me, following behind, a friendly wink as he gestured to the back of his truck. Painfully I climbed in and pulled the old tarpaulin over me. The truck moved on and stopped. The two men climbed out and one said, "We gotta load up a bit now, move forward." I crawled towards the driver's cab, and there was the clatter of boxes being loaded on.

The truck moved on, jolting over the rough roads. Soon it came to a halt, and a rough voice yelled, "What have you got there, folks?"

"Ouly garbage, sir," said the negro. Heavy footsteps came along beside me. Something poked about in the rubbish at the back. "Okay," said the voice, "on your way."

A gate clanged, the negro shifted into gear, and we drove out into the night. We seemed to drive for hours, then the truck turned sharply, braked, and came to a halt. The tarpaulin was pulled off, and there stood the Lascar and the negro, grinning down at me. I stirred wearily, and felt for my money. "I will pay you," I said.

"Pay nuthin'," said the negro.

"Butch was going to kill me before we reached New York," said the Lascar.

"You saved me, now I save you, and we put up a fight against the discrimination against us. Come on in."

"Race, creed, and colour do not matter," I thought. "All men bleed red." They led me into a warm room where there were two light coloured negro women. Soon I was wrapped in hot blankets, eating hot food. Then, they showed me a place where I could sleep, and I drifted off.

Chapter Seven

FOR two days and nights I slept, my exhausted body hovering between two worlds. Life had always been hard to me, always suffering and great misunderstanding. But now I slept.

My body was left behind me, left upon Earth. As I soared upwards I saw that one of the negro women was looking down at my empty shell with great compassion on her face. Then she turned away and sat by a window, looking out upon the dingy street. Freed of the fetters of the body, I could see even more clearly the colours of the astral. These people, these coloured people who were helping me when those of the white race could only persecute, were good. Suffering and hardships had refined their egos, and their insouciant attitude was merely to cover up their inner feelings. My money, all that I had earned by hardship, suffering and self-denial, was tucked beneath my pillow, as safe with these people as in the strongest bank.

I soared on and on, leaving the confines of time and space, entering astral plane after astral plane. At last I reached the Land of the Golden Light where my Guide, the Lama Mingyar Dondup waited to receive me.

"Your sufferings have been truly great," he said, "but all that you have endured has been to good purpose. We have studied the people of Earth, and the people of strange, mistaken cults there who have and will persecute you, for they have little understanding. But now we have to discuss your future. Your present body is nearing the end of its useful life, and the plans which we have for this event must come to pass." He walked beside me along the banks of a beautiful river. The waters sparkled and seemed to be alive. On either bank there were gardens so wonderful that I could scarce believe my senses. The air itself seemed to vibrate with life. In the distance a group of people, clad in Tibetan robes, came slowly to meet us. My guide smiled at me, "This is an important meeting," he said, "for we have to plan your future. We have to see how research into the human aura can be stimulated, for we have noticed that when 'aura 'is mentioned on Earth, most people try to change the subject."

The group moved nearer, and I recognized those of whom I had stood in awe. Now they smiled benevolently upon me, and greeted me as an equal. Let us move to more comfortable surroundings," said one, "so that we may talk and discuss matters at leisure." We moved along the path in the direction from whence the men had come until, turning to follow a bend in the path, we saw before us a Hall of such surpassing beauty that involuntarily I stopped with a gasp of pleasure. The walls seemed to be of purest crystal, with delicate pastel shades and undertones of colour, which changed as one looked. The path was soft under-foot, and it needed little urging on the part of my Guide to persuade me to enter.

We moved in, and it was as if we were in a great Temple, a Temple without dark, clean, with an atmosphere that simply made one feel that this was Life. Through the main body of the building we went, until we came to what on Earth I would have called the Abbot's room. Here there was comfortable simplicity, with a single picture of the Greater Reality upon the wall. Living plants were about the walls, and from the wide windows one could see across a superb expanse of parkland.

We sat upon cushions placed upon the floor, as in Tibet. I felt at home, contented almost. Thoughts of my body back on Earth still disturbed me, for so long as the Silver Cord was intact, I would have to return. The Abbot—I will call him that although he was much higher—looked about him, then spoke. "From here we have followed all that has happened to you upon the Earth. We want first to remind you that you are not suffering from the effects of Kharma, but are instead acting as our instrument of study. For all the bad that you now suffer, so shall you have your reward." He smiled at me, and added, "Although that does not help much when you are suffering upon Earth! However," he went on. "we have learned much, but there are certain aspects yet to be covered. Your present body has too much and will shortly fail. We have established a contact in the Land of England. This person wants to leave his body. We took him to the astral plane and discussed matters with him. He is most anxious to leave, and will do all we require. At our behest he changed his name to one more suitable to you. His life has not been happy, he willingly discontinued association with relatives. Friends he had never made. He is upon a harmonic of yours. For the moment we will not discuss him further, for later, before you take his body, you will see just a little of his life. Your present task is to get your body back to Tibet that it may be preserved. By your efforts and sacrifices you have amassed money, you need just a little more to pay your fare. It will come through your continued efforts. But enough for now. For a day enjoy your visit here before returning to your body."

This was bliss indeed, to be with my Guide, the Lama Mingyar Dondup, not as a child, but as an adult, as one who could appreciate that great man's unusual abilities and character. We sat alone on a mossy hillside overlooking a bay of bluest water. The trees swayed to a gentle breeze and wafted to us the scent of cedar and pine. For hours we stayed thus, talking, discussing the past. My history was an open book to him, now he told me of his. So the day passed, and as the purple twilight came upon me, I knew that it was time to go, time to return to the troubled Earth with its bitter man and spiteful tongues, tongues that caused the evils of Earth.

"Hank! Oh, Hank! He is awake!" There was the creak of a chair being moved, and as I opened my eyes I saw the big negro looking down at me. He was not smiling now, his face was full of respect, awe, even. The woman crossed herself and bowed slightly as she looked in my direction. "What is it? What has happened?" I asked.

"We have seen a miracle. All of us." The big negro's voice was hushed as he spoke.

"Have I caused you any trouble?" I asked.

"No, Master, you have brought us only joy," the woman replied.

"I would like to make you a present," I said, reaching for my money.

The negro spoke softly, "We are poor folk, but we will not take your money. Make this your home until you are ready to leave. We know what you are doing."

"But I would like to show my gratitude," I answered. "Without you I would have died."

"And gone to Greater Glory!" said the woman, adding, "Master, you can give us something greater than money. Teach us to pray!"

For a moment I was silent, taken aback by the request. "Yes," I said, "I will teach you to pray, as I was taught.

"All religions believe in the power of prayer, but few people understand the mechanics of the process, few understand why prayers work for some and seemingly not for others. Most Westerners believe that people of the East either pray to a graven image or do not pray at all. Both statements are untrue, and I am going to tell you now how you can remove prayer from the realm of mysticism and superstition and use it to help others, for prayer is a very real thing indeed. It is one of the greatest forces on this Earth when used as it was intended to be used.

"Most religions have a belief that each person has a Guardian Angel or

111

someone who looks after him. That also is true, but the Guardian Angel is oneself, the other self, the other self, which is at the other side of life. Very, very few people can see this angel, this Guardian of theirs, while they are on the Earth, but those who can are able to describe it in detail.

"This Guardian (we must call it something, so let us call it a Guardian) has not a material body such as we have on Earth. It appears to be ghostly; sometimes a clairvoyant will see it as a blue scintillating figure larger than life-size and connected to the flesh body by what is known as the Silver Cord, that Cord which pulses and glistens with life as it conveys messages from one to the other. This Guardian has not a body such as that of Earth, but it is still able to do things which the Earth body can do, with the addition that it can do very many more things which the Earth body cannot. For example, the Guardian can go to any part of the world in a flash. It is the Guardian which does astral travelling and relays back to the body through the Silver Cord that which is needed.

"When you pray, you pray to yourself, to your other self, to your Greater Self. If we knew properly how to pray we should send those prayers through the Silver Cord, because the telephone line we use is a very faulty sort of instrument indeed, and we have to repeat ourselves in order to make sure that the message gets through. So when you pray, speak as you would speak through a very long distance telephone line, speak with absolute clarity, and actually think of what you are saying. The fault, I should add, lies with us here on this world, lies with the imperfect body we have on this world, the fault is not in our Guardian. Pray in simple language making sure that your requests are always positive and never negative.

"Having framed your prayer to be absolutely positive and to be absolutely clear of any possibility of misunderstanding, repeat that prayer perhaps three times. Let us take an example; suppose, for instance, that you have a person who is ill and suffering, and you want to do something about it—you should pray for the relief of that person's suffering. You should pray three times saying exactly the same thing each time. You should visualize that shadowy figure, that insubstantial figure, actually going to the house of the other person, following the route which you would follow yourself, entering the house and laying hands on that person and so effecting a cure. I will return to this particular theme in a moment, but first let me say—repeat that as many times as are necessary, and, if you really believe, then there will be an improvement.

"This matter of a complete cure; well, if a person has a leg amputated, no amount of prayer will replace that leg. But if a person has cancer or any other grave disease, then that can be halted. Obviously the less the seriousness of the complaint, the easier it is to effect a cure. Everyone knows of the records of miracle cures throughout the history of the world. Lourdes and many other places are famed for their cures, and these cures are effected by the other self, by the Guardian of the person concerned in association with the fame of the locality. Lourdes, for example, is known throughout the world as a place for miracle cures so people go there utterly confident that they will be cured, and very often that confidence is passed on to the Guardian of the person and so a cure is effected very, very easily. Some people like to think that there is a saint or angel, or some ancient relic of a saint, that does the cure, but in reality each person cures himself and if a healer gets in touch with a person with the intention of curing that sick person, then a cure is effected only through the Guardian of that sick person. It all comes down, as I told you before, to yourself, the real self which you are when you leave this, the shadow life, and enter the Greater Reality. While upon Earth we all tend to think that this is the only thing that matters, but Earth, this world—no, this is the World of Illusion, the world of hardship, where we come to learn lessons not so easily learned in the kinder, more generous world to which we return.

"You may yourself have some disability, you may be ill, or you may lack the desired esoteric power. That can be cured, it can be overcome, if you believe it and if you really want it. Suppose you have a great desire, a burning desire, to help others; you may want to be a healer. Then pray in the seclusion of your private room, perhaps your bedroom. You should rest in the most relaxed position that you can find, preferably with your feet together and with your fingers interlinked, not m the usual attitude of prayer, but with your fingers interlinked. In that way you preserve and amplify the magnetic circuit of the body, and the aura becomes stronger, and the Silver Cord is able to convey messages more accurately. Then, having got yourself in the right position and in the right frame of mind, you should pray.

"You could pray, for example: 'Give me healing power that I may heal others. Give me healing power that I may heal others. Give me healing power that I may heal others.' Then have a few moments while you remain in your relaxed position, and picture yourself encompassed in the shadowy outline of your own body.

"As I told you before, you must visualize the route you would take to the sick person's house, and then make that body travel in your imagination to the home of that person you desire to heal. Picture yourself, your Overself, arrived at the house, arrived in the presence of the person you desire to help. Picture yourself putting out your arm, your hand, and touching that person. Imagine a flow of life-giving energy going along your arm, through your fingers, into that other person like a vivid blue light. Imagine that the person is gradually becoming cured. With faith, with a little practice, it can be done, it is being done, daily, in the Far East.

"It is useflil to place one hand in imagination on the back of the person's neck, and the other hand on or over the afflicted part. You will have to pray to yourself in groups of three prayers a number of times each day until you get the desired results. Again, if you believe, you will get results. But let me issue a grave, grave warning. You cannot increase your own fortune in this way. There is a very ancient occult law which stops one from profiting from prayers for self-gain. You cannot do it for yourself unless it is to help others, and unless you sincerely believe that it will help others. I know of an actual case wherein a man who had a moderate income and was fairly comfortably off, thought that if he won the Irish Sweepstake he would help others; he would be a great benefactor of mankind.

"Knowing a little, but not enough, of esoteric matters, he made great plans of what he would do. He set out with a carefully prepared programme of prayers. He prayed along the lines set out in this chapter for two months; he prayed that he would pick the winner of the Irish Sweepstake. For two months he prayed in groups of three prayers, three times a day—nine prayers in all during the day. As he fully anticipated, he won the Irish Sweepstake, and he won one of the biggest prizes of them all.

"Eventually he had the money and it went to his head. He forgot all about his good intentions, all about his promises. He forgot all about everything except that he had this vast sum of money and he could now do exactly as he wanted to do. He devoted the money to his own self-gratification. For a very few months he had a wonderful time, during which he became harder and harder, and then the inexorable law came into force, and instead of keeping that money and helping others, he lost everything that he had gained, and everything that he had before. In the end he died and was buried in a pauper's grave.

"I say to you that if you use the power of prayer properly, without thought of self-gain, without thought of self-aggrandizement, then you have tapped one of the greatest powers on Earth, a force so great that if just a few genuine people got together and prayed for peace, then there would be peace, and wars and thoughts of wars would be no more."

For some time after there was silence as they digested what I had told them, then the woman said, "I wish you would stay here awhile and teach us! We have seen a miracle, but Someone came and told us not to talk about it."

I rested for a few hours, then dressed and wrote a letter to my official friends in Shanghai, telling them what had happened to my papers. By airmail they sent me a fresh Passport which certainly eased my position. By airmail there arrived a letter from a very rich woman. "For some time," she wrote, "I have been trying to find your address. My daughter, whom you saved from the Japanese, is now with me and is completely restored to health. You saved her from rape and worse, and I want to repay, at least in part, our debt to you. Tell me what I can do for you."

I wrote to her and told her that I wanted to go home to Tibet to die. "I have enough money to buy a ticket to a port in India," I replied, "but not enough to cross that continent. If you really want to help me, buy me a ticket from Bombay to Kalimpong in India." I treated it as a joke, but two weeks later I received a letter and first class sea ticket and first class rail tickets all the way to Kalimpong. Immediately I wrote to her and expressed my gratitude, telling her that I intended giving my other money to the negro family who had so befriended me.

The negro family were sad that I was going to leave, but overjoyed that for once in my life I was going to have a comfortable journey. It was so difficult to get them to accept money. In the end we shared it between us! "There is one thing," said the friendly negro women. "You knew this money would come as it was for a good purpose. Did you send what you called a 'thought form' for it?"

"No," I answered, "it must have been accomplished by a source far removed from this world."

She looked puzzled. "You said that you would tell us about thought forms before you left. Will you have time now?"

"Yes," I replied. "Sit down, and I will tell you a story." She sat and folded her hands. Her husband turned out the light and sat back in his chair as I began to speak:

"By the burning sands, amid the grey stone buildings with the glaring sun overhead, the small group of men wended their way through the narrow streets. After a few minutes they stopped at a shabby looking doorway, knocked and entered. A few muttered sentences were uttered, and then the men were handed torches, which spluttered and sent drops of resin around. Slowly they made their way through corridors, getting lower and lower into the sands of Egypt. The atmosphere was cloying, sickly. It seeped into the nostrils, nauseating by the manner in which it clung to the mucous membrane.

115

"There was hardly a glimmer of light here except that which came from the torch bearers, the torch bearers who moved along at the head of the small procession. As they went further into the underground chamber the smell became stronger, the smell of Frankincense, of Myrrh, and of strange exotic herbs from the Orient. There was also the odour of death, of decay, and of decaying vegetation.

"Against the far wall was a collection of canopic jars containing the hearts and entrails of the people who were being embalmed. They were carefully labelled with the exact contents and with the date of sealing. These the procession passed with hardly a shudder, and went on past the baths of Nitre in which bodies were immersed for ninety days. Even now bodies were floating in these baths, and every so often an attendant would come along and push the body under with a long pole and turn it over. With scarcely a glance at these floating bodies, the procession went on into the inner chamber. There, resting upon planks of sweet smelling wood, was the body of the dead Pharaoh, wrapped tightly with linen bandages, powdered well with sweet smelling herbs, and anointed with unguents.

"The men entered, and four bearers took the body and turned it about, and put it in a light wooden shell which had been standing against a wall. Then, raising it to shoulder height, they turned and followed the torch bearers out of the underground room, past the baths of nitre, out of the rooms of the embalmers of Egypt. Nearer the surface the body was taken to another room where dim daylight filtered in. Here it was taken out of the crude wooden shell and placed in another one the exact shape of the body. The hands were placed across the breast and tightly bound with bandages. A papyrus was tied to them giving the history of the dead man.

"Here, days later, the priests of Osiris, of Isis, and of Horus came. Here they chanted their preliminary prayers conducting the soul through the Underworld. Here, too, the sorcerers and the magicians of old Egypt prepared their Thought Forms, Thought Forms which would guard the body of the dead man and prevent vandals from breaking into the tomb and disturbing his peace.

"Throughout the land of Egypt were proclamations of the penalties which would befall any who violated the tomb. The sentence: first the tongue of the violator would be torn out, and then his hands would be severed at the wrists. A few days later he would be disembowelled, and buried to the neck in the hot sand where he would live out the few short hours of life.

"The tomb of Tutankhamen made history because of the curse which fell upon those who violated that tomb. All the people who entered the tomb of Tutankhamen died or suffered mysterious, incurable illnesses.

"The priests of Egypt had a science which had been lost to the present-day world, the science of creating Thought Forms to do tasks which are beyond the skill of the human body. But that science need not have been lost, because anyone with a little practice, with a little perseverance, can make a thought form which will act for good or for bad.

"Who was the poet who wrote: 'I am the captain of my soul'? That man uttered a great truth, perhaps greater than he knew, for Man is indeed the captain of his soul. Western people have contemplated material things, mechanical things, anything to do with the mundane world. They have tried to explore Space, but they have failed to explore the deepest mystery of all—the sub-consciousness of Man, for Man is nine-tenths sub-conscious, which means that only one-tenth of Man is conscious. Only one-tenth of man's potential is subject to his volitional commands. If a man can be one and one-half-tenths conscious, then that man is a genius, but geniuses upon Earth are geniuses in one direction only. Often they are very deficient in other lines.

"The Egyptians in the days of the Pharaohs well knew the power of the sub-conscious. They buried their Pharaohs in deep tombs, and with their arts, with their knowledge of humanity, they made spells. They made Thought Forms which guarded the tombs of the dead Pharaohs and prevented intruders from entering, under penalty of dire disease.

"But you can make Thought Forms which will do good, but make sure they are for good because a Thought Form cannot tell good from evil. It will do either but the evil Thought Form in the end will wreak vengeance on its creator.

"The story of Aladdin is actually the story of a Thought Form which was conjured up. It is based upon one of the old Chinese legends, legends which are literally true.

"Imagination is the greatest force upon Earth. Imagination, unfortunately, is badly named. If one uses the word 'imagination' one automatically thinks of a frustrated person given to neurotic tendencies, and yet nothing could be further from the truth. All great artists, all great painters, great writers too, have to have a brilliant, controlled imagination, otherwise they could not visualize the finished thing that they are attempting to create.

"If we in everyday life would harness imagination, then we could achieve

117

what we now regard as miracles. We may, for example, have a loved one who is suffering from some illness, some illness for which as yet medical science has no cure. That person can be cured if one makes a Thought Form, which will get in touch with the Overself of the sick person, and help that Overself to materialize to create new parts. Thus, a person who is suffering from a diabetic condition could, with proper help, re-create the damaged parts of the pancreas which caused the disease.

"How can we create a Thought Form? Well, it is easy. We will go into that now. One must first decide what one wants to accomplish, and be sure that it is for good. Then one must call the imagination into play, one must visualize exactly the result which one wants to achieve. Supposing a person is ill with an organ invaded by disease. If we are going to make a Thought Form which will help, we must exactly visualize that person standing before us. We must try to visualize the afflicted organ. Having the afflicted organ pictorially before us, we must visualize it gradually healing, and we must impart a positive affirmation. So, we make this Thought Form by visualizing the person, we imagine the Thought Form standing beside the afflicted person and with super-normal powers reaching inside the body of that sick person, and with a healing touch causing the disease to disappear.

"At all times we must speak to the Thought Form which we have created in a firm, positive voice. There must not at any time be any suspicion of negativeness, nor of in decision. We must speak in the simplest possible language and in the most direct manner possible. We must speak to it as we would speak to a very backward child, because this Thought Form has no reason and can accept only a direct command or a simple statement.

"There may be a sore on some organ, and we must say to that Thought Form: 'You will now heal such-and-such an organ. The tissue is knitting together.' You would have to repeat that several times dally, and if you visuallze your Thought Form actually going to work, then it will indeed go to work. It worked with the Egyptians, and it can work with present-day people.

"There are many authenticated instances of tombs being haunted by a shadowy figure. That is because either the dead persons, or others, have thought so hard that they have actually made a figure of ectoplasm. The Egyptians in the days of the Pharaohs buried the embalmed body of the Pharaoh, but they adopted extreme measures so that their Thought Forms would be vivified even after thousands of years. They slew slaves slowly, painfully, telling the slaves that they would get relief from pain in the after-world if in dying they provided the necessary substance with which to make a substantial Thought Form. Archaeological records have long substantiated

118

hauntings and curses in tombs, and all these things are merely the outcome of absolutely natural, absolutely normal laws.

"Thought Forms can be made by anyone at all with just a little practice, but you must first at all times concentrate upon good in your Thought Form because if you try to make an evil form, then assuredly that Thought Form will turn upon you and cause you the gravest harm perhaps in the physical, in the mental, or in the astral state."

The next few days were frantic ones, transit visas to obtain, final preparations to be made, and things to be packed up and sent back to friends in Shanghai. My crystal was carefully packed and returned there for my future use, as were my Chinese papers, papers which, incidentally, quite a number of responsible people have now seen.

My personal possessions I kept to the absolute, consisting of one suit of clothing and the necessary change of underwear. Now trusting no officials, I had photographic copies made of everything, passport, tickets, medical certificates and all! "Are you coming to see me off?" I asked my negro friends.

"No," they replied. "We should not be allowed near because of the colour bar!".

The final day arrived, and I went by bus to the docks. Carrying my small case, and presenting my ticket, I was confronted with a demand as to the whereabouts of the rest of my luggage. "This is all," I replied. "I am taking nothing more."

The Official was plainly puzzled—and suspicious. "Wait here," he muttered, and hurried off to an inner office. Several minutes later he came out accompanied by a more senior official. "Is this all your luggage, sir?" the new man asked.

"It is," I replied.

He frowned, looked at my tickets, checked the details against entries in a book, and then stalked off with my tickets and the book. Ten minutes later he came back looking very disturbed. Handing me my tickets and some other papers, he said, "This is very irregular, all the way to India and no luggage!" Shaking his head he turned away. The former clerk apparently had decided to wash his hands of the whole affair, for he turned away and would not answer when I asked the location of the ship. Finally I looked at the new papers in my hand and saw that one was a Boarding Card giving all the required details.

It was a long walk to the ship's side and when I reached it I saw policemen lounging about but carefully watching passengers. I walked forward, showed my ticket and walked up the gangplank. An hour or so later two men came to my cabin and asked why I had no luggage. "But my dear man," I said "I thought this was the land of the free? Why should I be encumbered with luggage? What I take is my own affair surely?" He muttered and mumbled, and fiddled with papers and said, "Well we have to make sure that everything is all right. The clerk thought you were trying to escape from justice as you had no luggage. He was only trying to make sure."

I pointed to my case. "All I need is there; it will get me to India; in India I can pick up other luggage."

He looked relieved, "Ah! So you have other luggage, in India? Then that is all right."

I smiled to myself as I thought, "The only time I have trouble entering or leaving a country is when I do it legally, when I have all the papers Red Tape demands."

Life aboard the ship was dull, the other passengers were very class conscious and the story that I had brought "only one case!" apparently put me outside the range of human society. Because I did not conform to the snobbish norm I was as lonely as if I had been in a prison cell, but with the great difference that I could move about. It was amusing to see other passengers call a steward to have their deckchairs moved a little further away from me.

We sailed from the port of New York to the straits of Gibraltar. Across the Mediterranean Sea we steamed, calling at Alexandria, and then going on to Port Said, steaming along the Suez Canal to enter the Red Sea. The heat affected me badly, the Red Sea was almost steaming, but at last it came to an end, and we crossed the Arabian Sea to finally dock at Bombay. I had a few friends in that city, Buddhist priests and others, and I spent a week in their company before continuing my journey across India to Kalimpong. Kalimpong was full of Communist spies and newspaper men. New arrivals found their life was made a misery by the endless, senseless questioning, questions which I never answered but continued what I was doing. This penchant of Western people to pry into the affairs of others was a complete mystery to me, I really did not understand it.

I was glad to get out of Kalimpong and move into my own country, Tibet. I had been expected, and was met by a party of high lamas disguised as mendicant monks and traders. My health was deteriorating rapidly, and necessitated frequent stops and rest. At long last, some ten weeks later, we reached a secluded lamasery high in the Himalayas, overlooking the Valley of Lhasa, a lamasery so small and so inaccesible that Chinese Communists would not bother about it.

For some days I rested, trying to regain a little of my strength, rested, and meditated. I was home now, and happy for the first time in years. The deceptions and treachery of Western peoples seemed no more than an evil nightmare. Daily, little groups of men came to me, to tell me of events in Tibet, and to listen to me while I told them of the strange harsh world outside our frontiers.

I attended all the Services, finding comfort and solace in the familar rituals. Yet I was a man apart, a man who was about to die and live again. A man who was about to undergo one of the strangest experiences to fall to the lot of a living creature. Yet was it that strange? Many of our higher Adepts did it for life after life. The Dalai Lama himself did it, time after time taking over the body of a new-born baby. But the difference was, I was going to take over the body of an adult, and mould his body to mine, changing molecule by molecule the complete body, not just the ego. Although not a Christian, my studies at Lhasa had required me to read the Christian Bible and listen to lectures on it. I knew that in the Bible it was stated that the body of Jesus, the Son of Mary and Joseph, was taken over by the "Spirit of the Son of God" and became Christ. I knew too that the Christian priests had a Convention in the year sixty (A.D) to ban certain teachings of Christ. Reincarnation was banned, the taking over of the body of others was banned, together with many, many matters taught by Christ.

I looked out of my glassless window at the city of Lhasa so far below. It was hard to realize that the hated Communists were in charge there. So far they were trying to win over the young Tibetans by wonderful promises. We called it "The honey on the knife", the more one licked the "honey" the sooner the sharp blade revealed.Chinese troops stood on guard at the Pargo Kaling, Chinese troops stood at the entrances to our temples, like pickets at a Western-world strike, stood jeering at our ancient religion. Monks were being insulted, even manhandled, and the illiterate peasants and herdsmen were encouraged to do likewise.

Here we were safe from the Communists, safe in this almost unclimbable precipice. About us the whole area was honeycombed with caves, and there was but precipitous path wounding round the very edge of the cliffs, with a sheer drop of more than two thousand feet for those who slipped. Here, when venturing out in the open, we used grey robes which blended with the rock face. Grey robes which concealed us from the chance gaze of the Chinese using binoculars.

Far off I could see Chinese specialists with theodolites and measuring sticks. They crawled about like ants, placing pegs into the ground, making entries in their books. A monk crossed in front of a soldier, the Chinese jabbed at the monk's leg with his bayonet. Through the twenty magnification binoculars—my one luxury—which I had brought, I could see the spurt of blood and the sadistic grin on the face of the Chinese. These glasses were good, revealing the proud Potala and my own Chakpori. Something nagged at the back of my mind, something was missing. I refocused the binoculars and looked again. Upon the waters of the Serpent Temple Lake nothing stirred. In the streets of Lhasa no dogs nuzzled among refuse piles. No wildfowl, no dogs! I turned to the monk at my side. "The Communists had them all killed for food. Dogs do not work, therefore they shall not eat, said the Communists, but they shall do one service in providing food. It is now an offence to have a dog or cat or a pet of any kind." I looked in horror at the monk. An offence to keep a pet! Instinctively I looked again at the Chakpori. "What happened to our cats there?" I asked.

"Killed and eaten", was the reply.

I sighed and thought, "Oh! If only I could tell people the truth about Communism, how they really treat people. If only the Westerners wer not so squeamish!"

I thought of the community of nuns of whom I had heard so recently from a high lama who, upon his journey, had come across a lone survivor and heard her story before she died in his arms. Her community of nuns, she told him, had been invaded by a wild band of Chinese soldiers. They had desecrated the Sacred Objects and stolen all there was of value. The aged Superior, they had stripped and rubbed her with butter. Then they had set her alight and laughed and shouted with joy at her screams. At last her poor blackened body lay still upon the ground, and a soldier drew his bayonet the length of her body to make sure that she was dead.

Old nuns were stripped and red hot coals thrust into them so that they died in agony. Younger nuns were raped in front of each other, each being raped some twenty or thirty times during the three days that the soldiers stayed. Then they tired of the "sport", or were exhausted, for they turned upon the women in a last frenzy of savagery. Some women had parts cut off, some were slit open. Yet others were driven, still naked, out into the bitter cold.

A little party of monks who were travelling to Lhasa had come upon them and had tried to help them, giving the women their own robes, trying to keep the feeble light of life flickering. The Chinese Communist soldiers, also on the way to Lhasa, had come upon them and treated the monks with such savage brutality that such things could not be put into print. The monks, mutilated beyond hope of saving, had been turned loose, naked, bleeding, until they died from loss of blood. One woman alone had survived; she had fallen in a ditch and had been hidden by prayer flags which the Chinese had ripped from their posts. At long last, the lama and his attendant acolyte had come upon the gruesome scene and together had heard the full tale from the nun's dying lips.

"Oh! To tell the Western world of the terrors of Communism", I thought, but as I was to later to find, to my cost, one cannot write or talk of the truth in the West. All horrors must be smoothed over, all must have a patina of "decency". Are the Communists "decent" when they rape, mutilate and kill? If people of the West would listen to the true accounts of those who have suffered, they would indeed save themselves such horrors, for Communism is insidious, like cancer, and while people are prepared to think that this dreadful cult is merely different politics, then there is danger indeed for the peoples's of the world. As one who has suffered, I would say—show people in print and pictures (no matter how dreadful) what goes on behind these "Iron Curtains".

While I was ruminating upon these things, and spasmodically scanning the landscape before me, an aged man, bent and walking with a stick, entered my room. His face was lined with much suffering, and his bones stood out prominently, covered only by parchment-tight, withered skin. I saw that he was sightless and I rose to take his arm. His eye-sockets glared as angry red holes, and his movements were uncertain, as are those of the recently blinded. I sat him by me, and gently held his hand, thinking that here in this invaded land we had nothing now with which to alleviate his suffering and ease the pain of those inflamed sockets.

He smiled patiently and said, "You are wondering about my eyes, Brother. I was upon the Holy Way, making my prostrations at a Shrine. As I rose to my feet I gazed upon the Potala, and by a mischance a Chinese officer was in my line of sight. He charged that I was gazing upon him arrogantly, that I was looking at him offensively. I was tied by a rope to the end of its car and dragged along the ground to the square. There spectators were rounded up, and in front of them my eyes were gouged out and thrown at me. My body, as you can surely see, has many half-healed wounds. I was brought here by others and now I am glad to greet you."

I gasped with horror as he pulled open his robe, for his body was a raw red mass through being dragged along the road. I well knew this man. Under him, as an Acolyte, I had studied things of the mind. I had known him when I became a lama, for he had been one of my sponsors. He had been one of the lamas when I had journeyed far down beneath the Potala to endure the Ceremony of the Little Death. Now he sat beside me, and I knew that his death was not far off.

"You have travelled far and have seen and endured much," he said. "Now my last task in this Incarnation is to help you obtain glimpses, through the Akashic Record, of the life of a certain Englishman who is most anxious to depart his body that you may take over. You will glimpses only, for it takes much energy and we are both low in strength." He paused, and then, with a faint smile on his face, continued, "The effort will finish this present life of mine, and I am glad to have this oppertunity of acquiring merit through this last task. Thank you, Brother, for making this possible. When you return here from the Astral Journey, I shall be dead beside you."

The Akashic Record! What a wonderful source of knowledge that was. What a tragedy that people did not investigate its possibilities instead of meddling with atom bombs. Everything we do, everything that happens, is indelibly impressed upon the Akasha, that subtle medium which interpenetrates all matter. Every movement which has taken place on Earth since Earth first was, is available for those with the necessary training. To those with their "eyes" open, the history of the world lies before them. An old prediction says that after the end of this century scientists will be able to use the Akashic Record to look into history. It would be interesting to know what Cleopatra really said to Anthony, and what Mr. Gladstone's famous remarks were. To me it would be delightful to see my critics' faces when they saw what asses they really are, when they had to admit that I wrote the truth after all, but, sad to say, none of us will be here then.

But this Akashic Record, can we explain it more clearly? Everything that happens "impresses" itself upon that medium which interpenetrates even air. Once a sound has been made, or an action initiated, it is there for all time. With suitable instruments anyone could see it. Look at it in terms of light, or the vibrations, which we call light and sight. Light travels at a certain speed. As every scientist knows, we see stars at night which may no longer be in existence. Some of those stars are so very far away that the light from them

124

which is now reaching us may have started on its journey before this Earth came into being. We have no way of knowing if the star died a million or 50 years ago because the light would still reach us for perhaps a million more years. It might be easier to remind one of sound. We see the flash of lightning and hear the sound some time later. It is the slowness of sound, which makes for the delay in hearing it after seeing the flash. It is the slowness of light, which may make possible an instrument for "seeing" the past.

If we could move instantly to a planet so far distant that it took light one year to reach it from the planet which we had just left, we would see light which had started out one year before us. If we had some, as yet imaginary, super-powerful, super-sensitive telescope with which we could focus on any part of the Earth, we would see events on Earth which were a year old. Given the ability to move with our super telescope to a planet so far distant that the light from Earth took one million years to reach it, we should then be able to see Earth as it was one million years ago. By moving further and further, instantly, of course, we should eventually reach a point from which we would be able to see the birth of Earth, or even the sun.

The Akashic Record enables us to do just that. By special training we can move into the astral world where Time and Space do not exist and where other "dimensions" take over. Then one sees all. Other Time and Space? Well, as a simple example, suppose one had a mile of thin thread, sewing cotton if you like. One has to move from one side to the other. As things are on Earth we cannot move through the cotton, nor around its circumference. One has to travel all along the surface to the end a mile away, and back the other side, another mile. The journey is long. In the astral we should just move through. A very simple example, but moving through the Akashic Record is as simple, when one knows how!

The Akashic Record cannot be used for wrong purposes, used to gain information which would harm another. Nor without special dispensation, could one see and afterward discuss the private affairs of a person. One can, of course, see and discuss those things which are properly the affairs of history. Now I was going to see glimpses of the private life of another, and then I had to finally decide; should I take over this other body to substitute for mine? Mine was failing rapidly, and to accomplish my allotted task, I had to have a body to "tide me over" until I could change its molecules to mine.

I settled myself, and waited for the blind lama to speak.

125

Chapter Eight

SLOWLY the sun sank behind the distant mountain range, outlining the high peaks in the late effulgence. The faint spume streaming from the towering pinnacles caught the fading light and reflected a myriad of hues which changed and fluctuated with the vagaries of the soft evening breeze. Deep purple shadows stole from the hollows like creatures of the night coming out to play. Gradually the velvet darkness crept up along the base of the Potala, climbing ever higher, until only the golden roofs reflected a last gleam before they too were submerged in the encroaching darkness. One by one little glimmers of light appeared, like living jewels placed upon blackness for greater display.

The mountainous wall of the Valley stood out hard and austere, with the light behind it diminishing in intensity. Here, in our rocky home, we caught a last glimpse of the declining sun as it illuminated a rocky pass. Then we too were in darkness. No light for us, we were denied all for fear of betraying our sanctuary. For us there was naught but the darkness of the night and the darkness of our thoughts as we gazed upon our treacherously invaded land.

"Brother," said the blind lama, whose presence I had almost forgotten while thinking my own unhappy thoughts. "Brother, shall we go?" Together we sat in the lotus position and meditated upon that which we were going to do. The gentle night wind moaned softly in ecstasy as it played around the crags and pinnacles of rock and whispered in our window. With the not unpleasing jerk which so often accompanies such release, the blind lama—now blind no longer—and I soared from our earthly bodies into the freedom of another plane.

"It is good to see again," said the lama, "for one treasures one's sight only when it is gone." We floated along together, along the familiar path to that place which we termed the Hall of Memories. Entering in silence, we saw that others were engaged in research into the Akashic but what they saw was invisible to us, as our own scenes would be invisible to them.

"Where shall we start, Brother," said the old lama. "We do not want to intrude," I replied, "but we should see what sort of a man with whom we deal."

For a while there was silence between us as pictures sharp and clear formed for us to see. "Eek!" I exclaimed, jumping up in alarm. "He is married. What can I do about that? I am a celibate monk! I am getting out of this." I turned in great alarm and was stopped by the sight of the old man fairly shaking with laughter. For a time his mirth was so great that he simply could not speak.

"Brother, Lobsang," he managed to say at last, "you have greatly enlivened my declining days. I thought at first that the whole hierarchy of devils had bitten you as you sat, you jumped so high. Now, Brother, there is no problem at all, but first let me have a friendly 'dig' at you. You were telling me of the West, and of their strange beliefs. Let me quote you this, from their own Bible:

'Marriage is honourable in all' (Hebrews, Chapter Thirteen, Verse Four)." Once again he was attacked by a fit of laughter, and the more glumly I looked at him, the more he laughed, until in the end he stopped from exhaustion.

"Brother," he continued, when he was able, "those who guide us and help us had that in mind. You and the lady may live together in a state of companionship, for do not our own monks and nuns live at times under the same roof? Let us not see difficulties where none exist. Let us continue with the Record."

With a heart-felt sigh, I nodded dumbly. Words for the moment were quite beyond me. The more I thought of it all, the less I liked any of it. I thought of my Guide, the Lama Mingyar Dondup, sitting in comfort somewhere up in the Land of the Golden Light. My expression must have become blacker and blacker, for the old lama started laughing again.

At last we both calmed down and together watched the living pictures of the Akashic Record. I saw the man whose body it was hoped I would take. With increasing interest I observed that he was doing surgical fitting. To my delight it was obvious that he certainly knew what he was doing, he was a competent technician, and I nodded in involuntary approval as I watched him deal with case after case.

The scene moved on and we were able to see the city of London, in England, just as if we mingled with the crowds there. The huge red buses roared along the streets, weaving in and out of traffic and carrying great loads of people. A hellish shrieking and wailing broke out and we saw people dart for shelter in strange stone buildings erected in the streets. There was the incessant "crumpcrump" of anti-aircraft shells and fighters droned across the sky. Instinctively we ducked as bombs fell from one of the planes and whistled down. For a moment there was a hushed silence, and then whoom! Buildings leaped into the air and came down as dust and rubble.

Down in the deep subways of the underground railways, people were living a strange, troglodytic existence, going to the shelters at night, and emerging like moles in the morning. Whole families apparently lived there, sleeping upon makeshift bunks, and trying to obtain a little privacy by draping blankets from any available protrusion in the smooth tiled walls.

I seemed to be standing on an iron platform high above the roof-tops of London, with a clear view across to the building which people called "The Palace". A lone plane dived from the clouds, and three bombs sped down to the home of the King of England. I looked about me. When seeing through the Akashic Record one "sees" as did the principal character, so the old lama and I both saw as if both of us were the chief figure. It seemed to me that I was standing on a fire escape stretching across the roof-tops of London. I had seen such things before, but I had to explain the use of it to my companion. Then it dawned on me, he—the figure I was watching—was doing aircraft spotting in order to give warning to those below if imminent danger should threaten. The sirens sounded again, the All Clear, and I saw the man climb down and remove his Air Raid Warden's steel helmet.

The old lama turned to me with a smile, "This is most interesting, I have not watched events in the occident, my interests have been confined to our own country. I now understand what you mean when you say that 'one picture is worth a thousand words'. We must look again."

As we sat and watched the Record we saw the streets of London blacked out, with motor cars fitted with special headlamp shields. People bumped into posts and into each other. Inside the subway trains, before they came to the surface, the ordinary lights were switched off, and dismal blue bulbs were switched on. The beams of searchlights probed into the night sky, sometimes illuminating the grey sides of the barrage balloons. The old lama looked at the balloons in absolute fascination. Astral travelling he well understood, but these grey monsters, tethered on high, shifting restlessly in the night wind really amazed him. I confess that I found my companion's expression as interesting as the Akashic Record.

We watched the man get out of the train and walk along the darkened streets until he reached a large block of flats. We watched him enter, but did not enter with him; instead we looked at the busy scene outside. Houses were wrecked by bombs, and men were still digging in order to recover the living and the dead. The wail of the sirens interrupted rescue operations. Far up, like moths fluttering in the lamplight, enemy bombers were caught in a cross-cross of searchlight beams. Glinting light from one of the bombers attracted our curious gaze, and then we saw that the "lights" were the bombs on their way down. One dropped with a "crump" into the side of the big block of flats. There was a vivid flash and a shower of shattered masonry. People came pouring out of the building, came out into the doubtful safety of the streets.

"You have had worse than this, my Brother, in Shanghai?" asked the old lama.

"Much worse," I replied. "We had no defences and scant facilities. As you know, I was buried for a time in a wrecked shelter there, and escaped only with great difficulty."

"Shall we move on a little in time?" asked my companion. "We do not need to watch endlessly for we are both enfeebled in health."

I agreed with the utmost alacrity. I merely needed to know what sort of person it was from whom I was going to take over. For me there was no interest whatever in prying into the affairs of another. We moved along the Record, halted experimentally, and moved on again. The morning light was besmirched by the smoke of many fires. The night hours had been an inferno. It seemed that half London was ablaze. The man walked down the debris-littered street, a street that had been heavily bombed. At a temporary barricade a War Reserve policeman stopped him. "You cannot go any farther, sir, the buildings are dangerous." We saw the Managing Director arrive and speak to the man whose life we were watching. With a word to the policeman, they ducked under the rope and walked together to the shattered building. Water was spraying over all the stock from broken pipes. Plumbing and electric wires were inextricably entwined, like a skein of wool with which a kitten had played. A safe hung at a precarious angle still teetering on the very edge of a large hole. Sodden rags flapped miserably in the breeze, and from adjacent buildings flecks of burnt paper floated down like flakes of coal-black snow. I who had seen more of war and suffering than most, was still sickened by the senseless destruction. The Record went on...

Unemployment, in war-time London! The man tried to enlist as a War Reserve Policeman. Tried in vain. His medical papers were marked Grade Four, unfit for service. Now, with his employment gone, through the dropping of the bomb, he walked the streets in search of work. Firm after firm refused to take him. There seemed to be no hope, nothing to lighten the darkness of his hard times.

At last, through a chance visit to a Correspondence School with whom he had studied—and impressed them with his mental alertness and industry, he was offered employment at their war-time offices outside London. "It is a beautiful place," said the man who made the offer. "Go down on the Green Line bus. See Joe, he should be there by one, but the others will look after you. Take the Missus for the trip. I've been trying to get shifted there myself." The village was indeed a dump! Not the "beautiful place" he had been led to suppose. Aircraft were made there, tested, and flown to other parts of the country.

Life in a Correspondence College was boring indeed. So far as we could see, watching the Akashic Record, it consisted of reading forms and letters from people and then suggesting what Course of postal instruction they should take. My own personal opinion was that correspondence teaching was a waste of money unless one had facilities for practical work as well.

A strange noise like a faulty motor-cycle engine came to our ears. As we watched, a peculiar aeroplane came into view, a plane with no pilot or crew. It gave a spasmodic cough and the engine cut, the plane dived and exploded just above the ground. "That was the German robot plane," I said to the old lama, "The V.1 and the V.2 seem to have been unpleasant affairs." Another robot plane came over near the house in which the man and his wife lived. It blew windows in at one side of the house, and out at the other side and cracked a wall.

"They do not appear to have many friends," said the old lama "I think they have possibilities of the mind which the casual observer would overlook. It seems to me that they live together more as brother and sister than as husband and wife. That should comfort you, my Brother!" the old man said with quite a chuckle.

The Akashic Record went on, portraying a man's life at the speed of thought. We could yet move from one portion to another, ignoring certain parts or seeing other incidents time after time. The man found that a series of coincidences occurred which turned his thoughts more and more to the East. "Dreams" showed him life in Tibet, dreams which, really were astral travelling trips under the control of the old lama. "One of our very minor difficulties," the old man told me, "was that he wanted to use the word 'master' whenever he spoke to one of us."

"Oh!" I replied, "that is one of the common mistakes of the Western people, they love to use any name which implies power over others. What did you tell him?"

The old lama smiled and said, "I gave him a little talk, I also tried to get him to ask less questions. I will tell you what I said, because it is of use in deducing his inner nature. I said: That is a term which is most abhorrent to me and to all Easterners. 'Master' infers that one is seeking domination over others, seeking supremacy over those who have no right to use 'master'. A school master endeavours to inculcate learning in his pupils. To us 'Master' means Master of Knowledge, a source of knowledge, or one who has mastered the temptations of the flesh. We—I told him—prefer the word Guru, or Adept. For no Master, as we know the word, would ever seek to influence a student nor to impose his own opinions. In the West certain little groups and cults there are who think that they alone have the key to the Heavenly Fields. Certain religions used tortures in order to gain converts. I reminded him of a carving over one of our lamaseries—'a thousand monks, a thousand religions'.

"He seemed to follow my talk very well," said the old lama, "so I gave him a little more with the idea of striking while the iron was hot. I said: In India, in China, and in old Japan, the student-to-be will sit at the feet of his Guru seeking information, not asking questions, for the wise student never asks questions lest he be sent away. To ask a question is proof positive to the Guru that the student is not yet ready to receive answers to his questions. Some students have waited as long as seven years for information, for the answer to an unspoken question. During this time the student tends the bodily wants of the Guru, attends to his clothing, to his food, and to the few other needs that he has. All the time his ears are alive for information, because by receiving information, perhaps hearing that which is being given to other people, the wise student can deduce, can infer, and when the Guru in his wisdom sees that the student is making progress, that Guru, in his own good time, and in his own suitable way, questions the student, and if he finds some of the pupil's accumulated store of knowledge is faulty or incomplete, then the Guru, again in his own good time, repairs the omissions and deficiencies.

"In the West people say—'Now, tell me this. Madame Blavatsky said—Bishop Ledbetter says—Billy Graham says—What do you say?—I think you are wrong!' Westerners ask questions for the sake of talk, they ask questions not knowing what they want to say, not knowing what they want to hear, but when perhaps a kindly Guru answers a question, the student immediately argues and says, 'Oh well, I heard so-and-so say this, or that, or something else.'

"If the student asks a Guru a question, it must imply that the student does not know the answer, but considers that the Guru does, and if the student immediately questions the answer of the Guru, it shows that the student is ignorant and has preconceived and utterly erroneous ideas of decorum and of ordinary common decency. I say to you that the only way to obtain answers to your questions is, leave your questions unasked and collect information, deduce and infer, then in the fullness of time, provided you are pure in heart, you will be able to do astral travelling, and the more esoteric forms of meditation, and will thus be enabled to consult the Akashic Record which cannot lie, cannot answer out of context, and cannot give an opinion or information coloured by personal bias. The human sponge suffers from mental indigestion and sadly retards his or her evolution and spiritual development. The only way to progress? That is to wait and see. There is no other way, there is no way of forcing your development except at the express invitation of a Guru who knows you well, and that Guru, knowing you well, would soon speed your development if he thought that you were worthy."

It seemed to me that most Westerners would benefit by being taught that! But we were not here to teach, but to watch the unfolding of vital scenes from a man's life, a man who would shortly vacate his earthly shell.

"This is interesting," said the old lama, drawing my attention to a scene on the Record. "This took much arranging, but when he saw the desirability of it, he made no demur." I looked at the scene in some puzzlement, then it dawned upon me. Yes! That was a solicitor's office. That paper was a Change of Name Deed Poll. Yes, that was correct, I remembered, he had changed his name because that which he had had previously had the wrong vibrations as indicated by our Science of Numbers. I read the document with interest and saw that it was not quite correct, although it was near enough.

Of suffering there was plenty. A visit to a dentist caused much damage, damage which necessitated his removal to a nursing home for an operation. Out of technical interest, I watched the proceedings with considerable care.

He—the man whose life we were watching—felt that the employer was uncaring. We, watching, felt the same, and the old lama and I were glad the man gave notice of the termination of his engagement in the postal training school. The furniture was loaded on a van, some of it was sold, and the man and his wife left the area for an entirely fresh district. For a time they lived in the house of a strange old woman who "told fortunes", and had an amazing idea of her own importance. The man tried and tried to obtain employment. Anything which would enable him to earn money honestly.

The old lama said, "Now we are approaching the crucial part. As you will observe, he rails against fate constantly. He has no patience and I am afraid that he will depart his life violently unless we hurry."

132

"What do you wish me to do?" I asked.

"You are the senior," said the old man, "but I would like you to meet him in the astral, and see what you think."

"Certainly," was my rejoinder, "We will go together." For a moment I was lost in thought, then I said, "In Lhasa it is two o'clock in the morning. In England it will be eight o'clock in the evening, for their time lags behind ours. We will wait and rest for three hours, and will then draw him over to the astral."

"Yes," said the old lama. He sleeps in a room alone, so we can do it. For the present let us rest, for we are weary."

We returned to our bodies, sitting side by side in the faint starlight. The lights of Lhasa were extinguished now, and the only glimmers came from the habitations of monks and the brighter lights from Chinese Communist guard posts. The tinkling of the little stream outside our walls sounded unnaturally loud against the silence of the night. From high above came the rattling of a small shower of pebbles dislodged by the higher wind. They rattled and bounced by us, jarring loose bigger stones. Down the mountainside they rushed, to end in a noisy heap by a Chinese barracks. Lights flashed on, rifles were discharged into the air, and soldiers ran wildly around, fearing attack from the monks of Lhasa. The commotion soon subsided, and the night was peaceful and still once again.

The old lama laughed softly, and said, "How strange to me that the people beyond our land cannot understand astral travelling! How strange that they think all this is imagination. Could it not be put to them that even changing one's body for that of another is merely like a driver changing from one automobile to another? It seems inconceivable that a people with their technical progress should be so blind to the things of the spirit."

I, with much experience of the West, replied, "But Western people, except for a very small minority, have not the capacity for spiritual things. All they want is war, sex, sadism, and the right to pry into the affairs of others."

The long night wore on, we rested and refreshed ourselves with tea and tsampa. At last the first faint streaks of light shot across the mountain range behind us. As yet the valley at our feet was immersed in darkness. Somewhere a yak began to bellow as if sensing that a new day would soon be upon us. Five in the morning Tibetan time. About eleven o'clock by the time in England, I judged. Gently I nudged the old lama who was dozing lightly. "Time we went into the astral!" I said.

133

"It will be the last time for me," he replied, "for I shall not return to my body again."

Slowly, not hurrying at all, we again entered the astral state. Leisurely we arrived at that house in England. The man lay there sleeping, tossing a little, on his face there was a look of extreme discontent. His astral form was encompassing his physical body with no sign yet of separation.

"Are you coming?" I asked, in the astral. "Are you coming?" repeated the old lama. Slowly, almost reluctantly, the man's astral form rose above his physical body. Rose, and floated above it, reversed, head of astral to feet of physical, as one does. The astral body swayed and bobbed. The sudden roar of a speeding train nearly sent it back into the physical. Then, as though a sudden decision had been reached, his astral form tilted, and stood before us. Rubbing his eyes as one awakening from sleep, he gazed upon us.

"So you want to leave your body?" I asked.

"I do, I hate it here!" he exclaimed vehemently.

We stood looking at each other. He seemed to me to be much misunderstood man. A man who, in England, would not make his mark on life, but who in Tibet would have his chance. He laughed sourly, "So you want my body! Well, you will find your mistake. It does not matter what you know in England, it is who you know that matters. I cannot get a job, cannot even get unemployment benefit. See if you can do better!"

"Hush, my friend," said the old lama, "for you know not to whom you are speaking. Perhaps your truculence may have impeded you from obtaining employment."

"You will have to grow a beard," I said, "for if I occupy your body, mine will soon be substituted, and I must have a beard to hide the damage to my jaws. Can you grow a beard?"

"Yes, Sir," he replied, "I will grow a beard."

"Very well," I said. "I will return here in one month and will take over your body, giving you release, so that my own body may eventually replace that which I shall have taken. Tell me," I asked, "how were you first approached by my people?"

"For a long time, Sir," he said, "I have hated life in England, the unfairness of

134

it, the favouritism. All my life I have been interested in Tibet and Far East countries. All my life I have had 'dreams' in which I saw, or seemed to see, Tibet, China, and other countries which I did not recognize. Some time ago I had a strong impulse to change my name by legal deed, which I did"

"Yes," I remarked, "I know all about that, but how were you approached recently, and what did you see?"

He thought a bit, and then said, "To tell you that, I should have to do it in my own way, and some of the information I have seems to be incorrect in view of my later knowledge."

"Very well," was my reply, "tell it to me in your own way and we can correct any misconceptions later. I must get to know you better if I am to take your body, and this is one way of so doing."

"Perhaps I may start with the first actual 'contact'. Then I can collect my thoughts better." From the railway station up the road came the braking judder of a train, bringing late-comers back from the City of London. Shortly there came the sound of the train starting off again, and then 'the man' got down to his story while the old lama and I listened carefully.

"Rose Croft, Thames Ditton," he started, "was quite a nice little place. It was a house set back from the road with a garden in front, a small garden, and a much larger garden at the rear. The house itself had a balcony at the back which gave quite a good view across the countryside. I used to spend a lot of time in the garden, particularly in the front garden because for some time it had been neglected and I was trying to put it in order. The grass had been allowed to grow so that it was several feet high and clearing it had become a major problem. I had already cut half of it with an old Indian Gurkha knife. It was hard work because I had to get on my hands and knees and take swipes at the grass and sharpen the knife on a stone at every few strokes. I was interested also in photography, and for some time I had been trying to take a photograph of an owl which lived in an old fir tree nearby, a fir tree well encased in climbing ivy.

My attention was distracted by the sight of something fluttering on a branch not far above my head. I looked up and to my delighted surprise I saw a young owl there, flapping about, clutching at the branch, blinded by the bright sunlight. Quietly I put down the knife which I had been using and made my way indoors to fetch a camera. With that in my hands and with the shutter set, I made my way to the tree and silently, or as silently as I could, I climbed up to the first branch. Stealthily I edged along. The bird, unable to

135

see me in the bright light but sensing me, edged further away out towards the end. I, quite thoughtless of the danger, moved forward and forward, and with each movement of mine, the bird went further forward until it was almost at the end of the branch, which was now bending dangerously beneath my weight.

"Suddenly I made a precipitous movement and there was a sharp crack and the odorous smell of powdered wood. The branch was rotten and it gave beneath me. I catapulted head first towards the earth beneath me. I seemed to take an eternity to fall those few feet. I remember the grass never looked greener, it seemed larger than life, I could see each individual blade with little insects on it. I remember, too, a ladybird took off in fright at my approach, and then there was a blinding pain, and a flash as if of coloured lightning, and all went black. I do not know how long I lay a crumpled inert mass beneath the branches of the old fir tree, but quite suddenly I became aware that I was disengaging myself from the physical body, I was seeing things with a greater perception than ever before. Colours were new and startlingly vivid.

"Gingerly I got to my feet, and looked about me. To my horrified amazement I found that my body was lying prone upon the ground. There was no blood to be seen, but certainly there was evidence of a nasty bump just over the right temple. I was more than a little disconcerted, because the body was breathing stertorously and showing signs of considerable distress. 'Death,' I thought, 'I have died; now I shall never get back.' I saw a thin smoky cord ascending from the body, from the head of the body to me. There was no movement in the cord, no pulsation, and I felt sickening panic. I wondered what I should do. I seemed to be rooted to the spot in fear, or perhaps for some other reason. Then a sudden movement, the only movement in this strange world of mine, attracted my eye, and I nearly screamed, or should have screamed if I had had a voice. Approaching me across the grass was the figure of a Tibetan lama dressed in the saffron robe of the High Order. His feet were several inches from the ground, and yet he was coming to me steadily. I looked at him with utter stupefaction.

"He came towards me, stretching out his hand, and smiled. He said, 'You have nothing to fear. There is nothing here to worry you at all.' I had the impression that his words were in a different tongue from mine, Tibetan maybe, but I understood it, and yet I had heard no sound. There was no sound at all. I could not even hear the sound of the birds, or the whistling of the wind in the trees. 'Yes,' he said, divining my thoughts, 'we do not use speech, but telepathy. I am speaking to you by telepathy.' Together we looked at each other, and then at the body lying on the ground between us. The Tibetan looked up at me again, and smiled, and said, 'You are surprised at my

136

presence? I am here because I was drawn to you. I have left my body at this particular instant and I was drawn to you because your own particular life vibrations are a fundamental harmonic of one for whom I act. So I have come, I have come because I want your body for one who has to continue life in the Western world, for he has a task to do which brooks no interference.'

"I looked at him aghast. The man was mad saying that he wanted my body! So did I, it was my body. I wasn't having anyone take off my property like that. I had been shaken out of the physical vehicle against my wish, and I was going back. But the Tibetan obviously got my thoughts again. He said, 'What have you to look forward to? Unemployment, illness, unhappiness, a mediocre life in mediocre surroundings, and then in the not too distant future death and the start all over again. Have you achieved anything in life? Have you done anything to be proud of? Think it over.'

"I did think it over. I thought of the past, of the frustrations, the misunderstandings, the unhappiness. He broke in on me, 'Would you like the satisfaction of knowing that your Kharma had been wiped away, that you had materially contributed towards a job of the utmost benefit to mankind?' I said, 'Well, I don't know about that, mankind hasn't been too good to me. Why should I bother?'

"He said, 'No, on this Earth you are blinded to the true reality. You do not know what you are saying, but with the passage of time, and in a different sphere, you will become aware of the opportunities you have missed. I want your body for another.' I said, 'Well, what am I going to do about it? I can't wander about as a ghost all the time, and we can't both have the same body.'

"You see, I took all this absolutely literally. There was something compelling about the man, something absolutely genuine. I didn't question for one moment that he could take my body and let me go off somewhere else, but I wanted more information, I wanted to know what I was doing. He smiled at me, and said—reassuringly, 'You, my friend, shall have your reward, you shall escape your Kharma, shall go to a different sphere of activity, and you shall have your sins erased because of what you are doing. But your body cannot be taken unless you are willing.'

"I really did not like the idea at all. I had had my body some forty years, and I was quite attached to it. I didn't like the idea of anyone else taking my body and walking off with it. Besides, what would my wife say, living with a strange man and knowing nothing about it? He looked at me again, and he said, 'Have you no thought for humanity? Are you not willing to do something to redeem your own mistakes, to put some purpose to your own mediocre life? You will be the gainer. The one for whom I act will take over this hard life of yours.'

"I looked about me. I looked at the body between us, and I thought, 'Well, what does it matter? It's been a hard life. I'm well out of it.' So I said, 'All right, let me see what sort of place I will go to, and if I like it, I'll say yes' Instantly I had a glorious vision, a vision so glorious that no words could describe it. I was well satisfied, and I said I would be willing, very willing, to have my release and go as soon as possible."

The old lama chuckled and said, "We had to tell him that it was not that quick, that you would have to come and see for yourself before you made a final decision. After all, it was a happy release for him, hardship for you."

I looked at them both. "Very well," I finally remarked, "I will come back in a month. If you then have a beard, and if you then are sure beyond all doubt that you want to go through with this, I will release you and send you off on your own journey."

He sighed with satisfaction, and a beatific expression stole over his face as he slowly withdrew into the physical body. The old lama and I rose up, and returned to Tibet.

The sun was shining from a blue cloudless sky. Beside me, as I returned to my physical body, the empty shell of the old lama slumped lifeless to the floor. He, I reflected, had gone to peace after a long and honourable life. I— by the Holy Tooth of Buddha— what had I let myself in for?

Messengers went forth into the high mountain lands to the New Home carrying my written affirmation that I would do the task as requested. Messengers came to me, bringing me as a graceful gesture of friendship some of those Indian cakes, which had so often been my weakness when I was at the Chakpori. To all intents I was a prisoner in my mountain home. My request that I be permitted to steal down, even in disguise, for a last visit to my beloved Chakpori was denied me. "You may fall victim to the invaders, my brother," they told me, "for they are remarkably quick to pull the trigger if they have any suspicion."

"You are sick, Reverend Abbot," said another. "Should you descend the mountain side your health may not permit you to return. If your Silver Cord be severed, then the Task will not be accomplished."

The Task! It was so amazing to me that there was "a task" at all. To see the human aura was to me as simple as for a man with perfect sight to see a person standing a few feet away from him. I mused upon the difference between East and West, thinking how easy it would be to convince a Westerner of a new labour-saving food, and how easy it would be to convince an Easterner of something new in the realms of the mind.

Time slipped by. I rested extensively, more extensively than ever in my life before. Then, shortly before the month was up, shortly before I was to return to England, I had an urgent call to visit again the Land of the Golden Light

Seated in front of all those High Personages, I had the somewhat irreverent thought that this was like a briefing during the war days! My thought was caught by the others, and one of them smiled and said, "Yes, it is a briefing! And the enemy? The Power of Evil which would stop our task from being accomplished."

"You will meet much opposition and very much calumny," said one. 'Your metaphysical powers will not be altered or lost in any way during the change-over," said another.

"This is your last Incarnation," said my beloved Guide, the Lama Mingyar Dondup. "When you have finished this life you are taking over, you will then return Home—to us." How like my Guide, I thought, to end on a happy note. They went on to tell me what was going to happen. Three astral-travelling lamas would accompany me to England and would do the actual operation of severing one free from his Silver Cord, and attaching the other—me! The difficulty was that my own body, still in Tibet, had to remain connected as I wanted my own "flesh molecules" to be eventually transferred. So, I returned to the world and together with three companions journeyed to England in the astral state.

The man was waiting. "I am determined to go through with it," he said.

One of the lamas with me turned to the man and said, "You must allow yourself to full violently by that tree as you did when we first approached you. You must have a severe shake, for your Cord is very securely attached."

The man pulled himself a few feet off the ground and i then let go, falling to the earth with a satisfying 'thud' . For a moment it seemed as if Time itself stood still. A car which had been speeding along halted on the instant, a bird in full flight suddenly stopped motionless—and stayed in the air. A horse drawing a van paused with two feet upraised and did not fall. Then, motion came back into our perception. The car jumped into motion, doing about thirty-five miles an hour. The horse started to trot, and the bird hovering above flashed into full flight. Leaves rustled and twisted and the grass rippled into little waves as the wind swept across it.

Opposite, at the local Cottage Hospital, an ambulance rolled to a stop. Two attendants alighted, walked round to the back, and pulled out a stretcher upon which was an old woman. Leisurely the men manoeuvred into position and carried her into the hospital. "Ah!" said the man. "She is going to the hospital, I am going to freedom." He looked up the road, down the road, and then said "My wife, she knows all about this. I explained it to her and she agrees." He glanced at the house and pointed. "That's her room, yours are there. Now I'm more than ready."

One of the lamas grasped the astral form of the man and slid a hand along the Silver Cord. He seemed to be tying it as one ties the umbilical cord of a baby after its birth. "Ready!" said one of the priests. The man, freed of his connecting Cord, floated away in company with the priest who was assisting him: I felt a searing pain, an utter agony which I never want to feel again, and then the senior lama said, "Lobsang, can you enter that body? We will help you."

The world went black. There was an utterly clammy feeling of black-redness. A sensation of suffocating. I felt that I was being constricted, constrained in something too small for me. I probed about inside the body feeling like a blind pilot in a very complicated aeroplane, wondering how to make this body work. "What if I fail now?" I thought miserably to myself. Desperately I fiddled and fumbled. At last I saw flickers of red, then some green. Reassured, I intensified my efforts, and then it was like a blind being drawn aside. I could see! My sight was precisely the same as before, I could see the auras of people on the road. But I could not move.

The two lamas stood beside, me. From now on, as I was to find, I could always see astral figures as well as physical figures. I could also keep even more in touch with my companions in Tibet. "A consolation prize'," I often told myself, "for being compelled to remain in the West at all."

The two lamas were looking concernedly at my rigidity, at my inability to move. Desperately I strained and strained, blaming myself bitterly for not having tried to find out and master any difference between an Eastern body and a Western. "Lobsang! Your fingers are twitching!" called out one of the lamas. Urgently I explored and experimented. A faulty movement brought temporary blindness. With the help of the lamas I vacated the body again, studied it, and carefully re-entered. This time it was more successful. I could

140

see, could move an arm, a leg. With immense effort I rose to my knees, wavered and tottered, and fell prone again. As if I were lifting the whole weight of the world I rose shakily to my feet.

From the house came a woman running, saying, "Oh, what have you done now? You should come in and lie down." She looked at me and a startled expression came upon her face, and for a moment I thought she was going to scream in hysteria. She controlled herself, and put an arm round my shoulders and helped me across the grass. Over a little gravel path, up one stone step, and through a wooden doorway and into a small hallway. From thence it was difficult indeed, for there were many stairs to climb and I was as yet very uncertain and clumsy in my movements.

The house really consisted of two flats and the one, which I was to occupy, was the upper. It seemed so strange, entering an English home in this manner, climbing up the some-what steep stairs, hanging on to the rail to prevent myself from falling over backwards. My limbs felt rubbery, as if I lacked full control over them—as indeed was the case, for to gain complete mastery of this strange new body took some days. The two lamas hovered round, showing considerable concern, but of course there was nothing they could do. Soon they left me, promising to return in the small hours of the night.

Slowly I entered the bedroom which was mine, stumbling like a sleepwalker, jerking like a mechanical man. Gratefully I toppled over on to the bed. At least, I consoled myself, I cannot fly down now! My windows looked out on to both the front and the back of the house. By turning my head to the right I could gaze across the small front garden, on to the road, across to the small Cottage Hospital, a sight which I did not find comforting in my present state.

At the other side of the room was the window through which, by turning my head to the left, I could see the length of the larger garden. It was unkempt, coarse grass growing in clumps as in a meadow. Bushes divided the garden of one house from the next. At the end of the grassy stretch there was a fringe of straggly trees and a wire fence. Beyond I could see the outlines of farm buildings and a herd of cows grazing nearby.

Outside my windows I could hear voices, but they were such "English" voices that I found it almost impossible to understand what was being said. The English I had heard previously had been mostly American and Canadian, and here the strangely accented syllables of one of the Old School Tie Brigade baffled me. My own speech was difficult, I found. When I tried to speak I produced just a hollow croak. My vocal cords seemed thick, strange'.

141

I learned to speak slowly, and to visualize what I was going to say first. I tended to say "cha" instead of "j", making "chon" for John, and similar errors. Sometimes I could hardly understand what I was saying myself!

That night the astral travelling lamas came again and cheered away my depression by telling me that now I should find astral travelling even easier. They told me, too, of my lonely Tibetan body safely stored in a stone coffin, under the unceasing care of three monks. Research into old literature, they told me, showed that it would be easy to let me have my own body, but that the complete transfer would take a little time.

For three days I stayed in my room, resting, practising movements, and becoming accustomed to the changed life. On the evening of the third day I walked shakily into the garden, under cover of darkness. Now, I found, I was beginning to master the body, although there were unaccountable moments when an arm or a leg would fail to respond to my commands.

The next morning the woman who was now known as my wife said, "You will have to go to the Labour Exchange today to see if they have any job for you yet" Labour Exchange? For some time it conveyed nothing to me, until she used the term "Ministry of Labour" then it dawned on me. I had never been to such a place and had no idea of how to behave or what to do there. I knew, from the conversation, that it was some place near Hampton Court but the name was Molesey.

For some reason which I did not then comprehend, I was not entitled to claim any unemployment benefit. Later I found that if a person left his employment voluntarily, no matter how unpleasant or unreasonable that employment, he was not entitled to claim benefit, not even if he had paid into the fund for twenty years.

Labour Exchange! I said, "Help me get the bicycle, and I will go." Together we walked down the stairs, turned left to the garage now stuffed with old furniture, and there was the bicycle, an instrument of torture which I had used only once before, in Chungking, where I had gone flying down the hill before I could find the brakes. Gingerly I got on the contraption and wobbled off along the road towards the railway bridge, turning left at the forked road. A man waves cheerily, and waving back, I almost fell off. "You don't look at all well," he called. "Go carefully!"

On I pedalled, getting strange pains in the leg. On, and turned right, as previously instructed, into the wide road to Hampton Court. As I rode along, my legs suddenly failed to obey my commands, and I just managed to free-wheel across the road to tumble in a heap, with the bicycle on top of me, on a stretch of grass beside the road. For a moment I lay there, badly shaken, then a woman who had been doing something to her mats outside her front door came storming down the path, yelling, "You ought to be ashamed of yourself, drunk at this time of the day. I saw you. I've a mind to ring up the police!" She scowled at me, then turned and dashed back to her house, picked up the mats and slammed the door behind her.

"How little she knows!" I thought. "How little she knows!"

For perhaps twenty minutes I lay there, recovering. People came to their doors and stared out. People came to their windows and peered from behind curtains. Two women came to the end of their gardens and discussed me in loud, raucous voices. Nowhere did I detect the slightest thought that I might be ill or in need of attention.

At last, with immense effort, I staggered to my feet, mounted the bicycle, and rode off in the direction of Hampton Court.

Chapter Nine

The exchange was a dismal house in a side street. I rode up, dismounted, and started to walk in the entrance. "Want your bike stolen?" asked a voice behind me. I turned to the speaker. "Surely the unemployed do not steal from each other?" I asked.

"You must be new around here; put a lock and chain round the bike or you will have to walk home." With that the speaker shrugged his shoulders and went into the building. I turned back and looked in the saddle-bag of the machine. Yes, there was a lock and chain. I was just going to put the chain round the wheel as I had seen others do when a horrid thought struck me— where was the key? I fumbled in those unfamiliar pockets and brought out a bunch of keys. Trying one after the other, I eventually found the correct one.

I walked up the path and into the house. Cardboard signs with black inked arrows pointed the way. I turned right and entered a room where there were a lot of hard wooden chairs packed tightly together.

"Hello, Prof!" said a voice. "Come and sit by me and wait your turn."

I moved to the speaker and pushed my way to a chair beside him. "You look different this morning," he continued. "What have you been doing to yourself?"

I let him do the talking, picking up stray bits of information. The clerk called names, and men went up to his desk and sat before him. A name was called which seemed vaguely familiar. "Someone I know?" I wondered. No one moved. The name was called again. "Go on—that's you!" said my new friend. I rose and walked to the desk and sat down as I had seen the others do.

"What's the matter with you this morning?" asked the clerk. "I saw you come in, then I lost sight of you and thought you had gone home." He looked at me carefully.

"You look different this morning, somehow. Can't be hair style, because you haven't any hair." Then he straightened up and said, "No, nothing for you, I'm afraid. Better luck next time. Next, please."

I walked out, feeling despondent, and cycled back to Hampton Court. There

144

I bought a newspaper, and continued on to the banks of the Thames. This was a beauty spot, a place where Londoners came for a holiday. I sat down on the grassy bank, with my back to a tree, and read the Situations Vacant columns in the paper.

"You'll never get a job through the Exchange!" said a voice, and a man came off the path and plonked down on the grass beside me. Plucking a long-stemmed grass, he chewed it reflectively, rolling it from side to side of his mouth. "They don't pay you any dole, see? So they don't get you fixed up either. They gives the jobs to them as what they has to pay. Then they save money, see? If they get you a job they have to keep somebuddy else on the dole and the Gov'ment makes a fuss, see?"

I thought it over. It made sense to me, even if the man's grammar almost made my head swim. "Well, what would you do?" I asked.

"Me! Blimey, I don't want no job, I just goes to get the dole, it keeps me, that an' a bit I makes on the side, like. Well, Guv. If you really want a job, go to one of them Bureys—here—let's have a look." He reached over and took my paper, leaving me to wonder blankly what a Burey could be. What a lot there was to learn, I thought. How ignorant I was of everything to do with the Western world. Licking his fingers, and mumbling the letters of the alphabet to himself, the man fumbled through the pages. "Here y'are!" he exclaimed triumphantly. "Employment Bureys —here—take a look at it yerself."

Quickly I scanned the column so clearly indicated by his very dirty thumb mark. Employment Bureaux, Employment Agencies. Jobs. "But this is for women," I said disgustedly.

"Garn!" he replied, "You can't read, it says there men and women. Now you go along an' see 'em an' don't take no old buck from them. Oh! They'll play you up and string you along if you let 'em. Tell 'em you want a job, or else!"

That afternoon I hurried off to the heart of London, climbing the dingy stairs to a ramshackle office in a back street of Soho. A painted woman with artificially blond hair and scarlet talons of nails was sitting at a metal desk in a room so small it might once have been a cupboard. "I want a job," I said.

She leaned back and surveyed me coolly. Yawning widely, she displayed a mouthful of decayed teeth and a furred tongue. "Ooaryer?" she said. I gaped at her blankly. "Ooaryer?" she repeated.

"I am sorry," I said, "but I do not understand your question."

145

"Oogawd!" she sighed wearily. "Ee don't speak no English. 'Ere fillupaform." She threw a questionnaire at me, removed her pen, clock, a book and her handbag, and disappeared into some back room. I sat down and struggled with the questions. At long last she reappeared and jerked her thumb in the direction from whence she had come. "Git in there," she commanded. I rose from my seat and stumbled into a little larger room. A man was sitting at a battered desk untidily littered with papers. He was chewing on the butt of a cheap and stinking cigar, a stained trilby hat was perched on the back of his head. He motioned for me to sit in front of him.

"Got yer Registration money?" he asked. I reached in my pocket and produced the sum stated on the form. The man took it from me, counted it twice, and put it in his pocket. "Where you bin waitin'?" he asked.

"In the outer office," I replied innocently. To my consternation he broke out into great guffaws of laughter.

"Hor! Hor! Hor!" he roared. "I said, 'Where you bin waitin'?' and 'e sezs 'in th' outer office'!" Wiping his streaming eyes, he controlled himself with a visible effort, and said, "Look, Cock, you ain't 'alf a comic, but I ain't got no time to waste. 'Ave you bin a waiter or aincha?"

"No," I replied. "I want employment in any of these lines"—giving him a whole list of things I could do—"now, can you help or can you not?"

He frowned as he looked at the list. "Well, I dunno," he said doubtfully, "you speak like a dook . . . look, we'll see what we can do. Come in a week today." With that, he relit his now extinguished cigar, parked his feet on the desk as he picked up a racing paper and started to read. I made my disillusioned way out, past the painted woman who greeted my departure with a haughty stare and a sniff, down the creaking stairs and into the dismal street.

Not far away there was another agency, and to it I made my way. My heart sank at the sight of the entrance. A side door, bare wooden stairs, and dirty walls with the paint peeling off Upstairs, on the second floor, I opened a door marked ' enter '. Inside was one large room, extending the width of the building. Rickety tables stood about and at each one sat a man or a woman with a pile of index cards in front.

"Yes? What can I do for you?" asked a voice at my side. Turning I saw a woman who might have been seventy, although she looked older. Without waiting for me to say anything, she handed me a questionnaire with the request that I complete it and hand it to the girl at the desk. I soon filled in all the numerous and very personal details and then took it to the girl as directed. Without a glance at it she said, "You may pay me your registration fee now." I did so thinking that they had an easy way of making money. She counted the money carefully, passed it through a hatch to another woman who also counted it, then I was given a receipt. The girl stood up and called, "Is anyone free?" A man at a desk in the far distance lethargically waved a hand. The girl turned to me and said, "That gentleman over there will see you." I walked over to him, threading my way between desks. For some time he took no notice of me but went on writing, then he held out his hand. I took it, and shook it, but he snatched it away crossly, saying irritably, "No, no! I want to see your Receipt, your Receipt, you know." Scrutinizing it carefully, he turned it over, and examined the blank side. Re-reading the front side, he apparently decided that it was genuine after all for he said, "Will you take a chair?"

To my amazement he took a fresh form, and asked me the answers to all the questions which I had just written. Dropping my completed form in the waste-paper basket, and his in a drawer, he said, "Come to me in a week's time and we will see what we can do." He resumed his writing, writing which I could see was a personal letter to some woman!

"Hey!" I said loudly, "I want attention now."

"My dear fellow!" he expostulated, "We simply cannot do things so hurriedly, we must have system, you know, system!"

"Well," I said, "I want a job now, or my money back."

"Dear, dear!" he sighed. "How perfectly ghastly!" With a quick glance at my determined face, he sighed again, and began pulling out drawer after drawer, as if stalling for time while he thought what to do next. One drawer he pulled too far. There was a crash and all sorts of personal belongings scattered on the floor. A box of some thousand paper clips spilled open. We scrabbled about on the floor, picking up things and tossing them on the desk.

At last everything was picked up and swept into the drawer. "That blawsted drawer!" he said resignedly, "Always slipping out of place like that, the other wallahs are used to it." For some time he sat there, going through his File Cards, then looking up bundles of papers, shaking his head negatively as he tossed them back and removing another bundle. "Ah!" he said at last, then fell silent. Minutes later, he said, "Yes, I have a job for you!"

He rifled through his papers, changed his spectacles and reached out blindly

147

towards a pile of cards. Picking up the top one he placed it in front of him and slowly began to write. "Now where is it? Ah! Clapham, do you know Clapham?" Without waiting for a reply, he continued, "It is a photographic processing works. You will work by night. Street photographers in the West End bring in their stuff at night and collect the proofs in the morning. H'mm yes, let me see." He went on fumbling through the papers, "You will sometimes have to work in the West End yourself with a camera as a relief man. Now take this card to that address and see him," he said, pointing with his pencil to a name he had written on the card.

Clapham was not one of the most salubrious districts of London; the address to which I went, in a mean back street in the slums adjacent to the railway sidings, was an ill-favored place indeed. I knocked at the door of a house which had the paint peeling off, and one window of which had the glass "repaired" with sticky paper. The door opened slightly and a slatternly woman peered out, tousled hair falling over her face.

"Yeh? 'Oo d'ye want?" I told her and she turned without speaking and yelled, "'Arry! Man to see ye!" Turning she pushed the door shut, leaving me outside. Sometime later the door opened, and a rough looking man stood there, unshaven, no collar, cigarette hanging from his lower lip. His toes showed through great holes in his felt slippers.

"What d'ye want, Cock?" he said. I handed him the card from the Employment Bureau. He took it, looked at it from all angles, looked from the card to me and back again, then said, "Furriner, eh? Plenty of 'em in Clapham. Not so choosey as us Britishers."

"Will you tell me about the job?" I asked.

"Not now!" he said, "I've got to see you fust. Come in, I'm in the bismint."

With that he turned and disappeared! I entered the house in a considerably fuddled state of mind. How could he be in the "bismint" when he had been in front of me, and what was the "bismint" anyhow?

The hall of the house was dark. I stood there not knowing where to go, and I jumped as a voice yelled beside me, seemingly at my feet, "Hi Cock, ain't'cha comin' dahn?"

A clatter of feet, and the man's head appeared from a dimly lit basement door which I had not noticed. I followed him down some rickety wooden stairs, fearing that any moment I would fall through. "The woiks!" the man said, proudly.

148

A dim amber bulb shone through a haze of cigarette smoke. The atmosphere was stifling. Along one wall was a bench with a drain running through its length. Photographic dishes stood at intervals along it. On a table off to the side stood a battered enlarger, while yet another table, covered in lead sheet, contained a number of large bottles.

"I'm 'Arry," said the man, "Make up yer solutions so I kin see how yer shape." As an afterthought, he added "We always use Johnson's Contrasty, brings 'em up real good." 'Arry stood aside, striking a match on the seat of his trousers so that he could light a cigarette. Quickly I made up the solutions, developer stop-bath, and fixer.

"Okay," he said. "Now get a holt of that reel of film and run off a few proofs. I went to make a test-strip, but he said, "No, don't waste paper, give'em five seconds."

'Arry was satisfied with my performance. "We pays monthly, Cock," he said. "Don't do no noods. Don't want no trouble with the cops. Give all the noods to me. The boys sometimes gets ideas and slips in special noods for special customers. Pass 'em all to me, see? Now you starts here at ten tonight and leaves at seven in the mornin, Okay? Then it's a deal!"

That night, just before ten, I walked along the dingy street, trying to see the numbers in the all-pervading gloom. I reached the house and climbed the untidy steps to the scarred and blistered door. Knocking, I stepped back and waited. But not for long. The door was flung open with a creak from its rusted hinges. The same woman was there, the one who had answered my knock earlier. The same woman, but what a different woman. Her face was powdered and painted, her hair was carefully waved and her almost transparent dress, with the hall light behind her, showed her plump form in clear detail. She directed a wide, tooth smile at me and said, "Come in Dearie. I'm Marie. Who sent you?" Without waiting for my reply, she bent over towards me her low-cut dress sagging dangerously, and continued, "It's thirty shillings for half an hour, or three pun' ten for the whole night. I know tricks, Dearie!"

As she moved to permit me to enter, the hall light shone upon my face. She saw my beard and glowered at me. "Oh, it's you!" she said frostily, and the smile was wiped from her face as chalk is wiped from a blackboard by a wet rag. She snorted, "Wasting my time! The very idea of it! Here, you," she bawled, "you will have to get a key, I'm usually busy at this time o'night."

I turned, shut the street door behind me, and made my way down to the dismal basement. There were stacks of cassettes to be developed, it seemed to me that all the photographers in London had dumped their films here. I worked in the Stygian darkness unloading cassettes, fixing clips to one end and inserting them in the tanks. "Clack-clack-clack" went the timer clock. Quite suddenly the timer bell went off, to tell me that the films were ready for the stop bath. The unexpected sound made me leap to my feet and bump my head against a low beam. Out with all the films, into the stop bath for a few minutes. Out again and into the fixing bath for a quarter of an hour. Another dip, this time in hypo eliminator, and the films were ready for washing. While this was being done, I switched on the amber light and enlarged up a few proofs.

Two hours later I had the films all developed, fixed, washed, and quick-dried in methylated spirits. Four hours on, and I was making rapid progress with the work. I was also becoming hungry. Looking about me, I could see no means of boiling a kettle. There wasn't even a kettle to boil, anyway, so I sat down and opened my sandwiches and carefully washed a photographic measure in order to get a drink of water. I thought of the woman upstairs, wondering if she was drinking beautiful hot tea, and wishing that she would bring me a cup.

The door at the head of the basement stairs was flung open with a crash, letting in a flood of light. Hastily I jumped up to cover an opened packet of printing paper before the light spoiled it, as a voice bawled, "Hey! You there! Want a cuppa? Business is bad tonight and I just made meself a pot before turning in. Couldn't get you out of my mind. Must have been telepathy." She laughed at her own joke and clattered down the stairs. Putting down the tray, she sat on the wooden seat, exhaling noisily.

"Phew!" she said, "Ain't 'alf 'ot down here." She undid the belt of her dressing-gown, pulled it open—and to my horror she had nothing on beneath! She saw my look and cackled, "I'm not trying for you, you've got other developments on your hands tonight." She stood up, her dressing-gown falling to the ground, and reached for the stack of drying prints. "Gee!" she exclaimed, leafing through them, "What mugs. Don't know why these geezers have their pictures took." She sat down again, apparently abandoning her dressing-gown without regret—it was hot here, and I was getting hotter!

"Do you believe in telepathy?" she asked.

"Of course I do!" I replied.

"Well I saw a show at the Palladium and they did telepathy there. I said it was genuine, but the fellow who took me said it was all a fake." . . .

150

There is an oriental legend about a traveler on the wide Gobi desert, his camel had died, and the man was crawling along, almost dying of thirst. Ahead of him he suddenly saw what appeared to be a waterskin, a goatskin filled with water which travelers carry. Hurrying desperately to the skin, he bent down to drink, and found it was merely a skin stuffed with first class diamonds which some other thirsty traveler had thrown away to lighten his load. Such is the way of the West, people seek material riches, seek technical advancement, rockets with bigger and better bangs, pilotless aircraft, and attempted investigation in space. The real values, astral traveling, clairvoyance, and telepathy they treat with suspicion, believing them to be fakes or comic stage turns.

When the British were in India it was well known that the Indians could send messages long distances, telling of revolts, impending arrivals, or any news of interest. Such messages would travel the country in mere hours. The same thing was noticed in Africa and was known as the "Bush telegraph". With training, there need be no telegraph wires! No telephones to jangle our nerves. People could send messages by their own innate abilities. In the East there have been centuries of study into such matters; Eastern countries are "sympathetic" to the idea and there is no negative thought to impede the working of the gifts of Nature.

"Marie," I said, "I will show you a little trick which demonstrates telepathy, or Mind over Matter. I being the Mind, you being the Matter."

She looked at me suspiciously, even glowered for a moment, and then replied, "Orlright, anything for a lark." I concentrated my thoughts on the back of her neck, imagining a fly biting her. I visualized the insect biting. Suddenly Marie swatted the back of her neck using a very naughty word to describe the offending insect. I visualized the bite being stronger, and then she looked at me and laughed. "My!" she said, "If I could do that I certainly would have some fun with the fellows who visit me!"

For night after night I went to the slovenly house in that drab back street. Often, when Marie was not busy, she would come with a teapot of tea to talk and to listen. Gradually I became aware that beneath her hard exterior, in spite of the life which she led, she was a very kind woman to those in need. She told me about the man who employed me and warned me to be at the house early on the last day of the month.

Night after night I developed and printed and left everything ready for an early morning collection. For a whole month I saw no one but Marie, then on the thirty-first, I stayed on late. About nine o'clock a shifty-looking individual came clattering down the uncarpeted stairs. He stopped at the bottom, and looked at me with open hostility. "Think you are going to get paid first, eh?" he snarled. "You are night man, get out of here!"

"I will go when I am ready, not before," I answered.

"You—!" he said, "I'll teach you to give me none of yer lip!"

He snatched up a bottle, knocked off the neck against a wall, and came at me with the raw, jagged edge aimed straight at my face. I was tired, and quite a little cross. I had been taught fighting by some of the greatest Masters of the art in the East. I disarmed the measley little fellow—a simple task—and put him across my knees, giving him the biggest beating he had ever had.

Marie, hearing the screams, dashed out from her bed and now sat on the stairs enjoying the scene! The fellow was actually weeping, so I shoved his head in the print-washing tank in order to wash away his tears and stop the flow of obscene language. As I let him stand up, I said, "Stand in that corner. If you move until I say you may, I will start all over again!" He did not move.

"My! That was a sight for sore eyes," said Marie. "The little runt is a leader of one of the Soho gangs. You have got him frightened, thought he was the greatest fighter ever, he did!"

I sat and waited. About an hour later, the man who had employed me came down the stairs, turning pale as he saw me and the gangster. "I want my money," I said. "It's been a poor month, I haven't any money, I have had to pay Protection to him," he said, pointing to the gangster.

I looked at him. "D'you think I'm working in this stinking hole for nothing?" I asked.

"Give me a few days and I'll see if I can rake some up. He"—pointing to the gangster—"takes all my money because if I don't pay him he gets my men in trouble."

No money, not much hope of getting any, either! I agreed to continue for another two weeks to give "the Boss" time to get some money somewhere. Sadly I left the house, thinking how fortunate it was that I cycled to Clapham in order to save fares. As I went to unchain my cycle, the gangster sidled furtively up to me. "Say, Guv'," he whispered hoarsely, "d'ye want a good job? Lookin' arter me. Twenty quid a week, all found."

"Get out of it, you runny-nosed little squirt," I answered dourly.

"Twenty-five quid a week!"

As I turned toward him in exasperation he skipped nimbly away, muttering, "Make it thirty, top offer, all the wimmin you want, and the booze you kin drink, be a sport!"

At the sight of my expression he vaulted over the basement railing and disappeared into somebody's private rooms. I turned, mounted the bicycle, and rode off.

For nearly three months I kept the job, doing processing and then having a turn on the streets as street-photographer, but neither I nor the other men got paid. At last, in desperation, we all finished.

By now we had moved to one of those dubious Squares in the Bayswater district, and I visited Labor Exchange after Labor Exchange in an attempt to get work. At last, probably in order to get rid of me, one official said, "Why don't you go to the Higher Appointments branch, at Tavistock Square? I'll give you a card." Full of hope I went to Tavistock Square. Wonderful promises were made to me. Here is one of them:

"By Jove, yes, we can suit you exactly, we want a man for a new atom research station in Caithness, in Scotland. Will you go up for an interview?" Industriously he raked among his papers.

I replied, "Do they pay traveling expenses?"

"Oh! Dear dear no!" was the emphatic reply, "You will have to go at your own expense."

On another occasion I traveled—at my own expense—to Cardigan in Wales. A man with a knowledge of civil engineering was required. I traveled, at my own expense, across England and into Wales. The Station was a shocking distance from the place of interview. I trudged through the streets of Cardigan and reached the other side. "My, my! It is indeed a long way yet, look you!" said the pleasant woman of whom I sought directions. I walked on, and on, and at last reached the entrance to a house hidden by trees. The drive was well kept. It was also very long; uphill. At last I reached the house. The amiable man whom I saw looked at my papers (which I had had sent to me in England from Shanghai). He looked, and nodded approvingly. "With papers such as these you should have no difficulty in gaining employment," he said. "Unfortunately you have no experience in England on civil engineering contracts. Therefore I cannot offer you an appointment. But tell

153

me," he asked, "You are a qualified doctor, why did you also study Civil Engineering? I see you have a Bachelor's degree in Civil Engineering."

"As a medical man, I was going to travel to remote districts, and I wanted to be able to build my own hospital," I said.

"H'mmph!" he grunted, "I wish I could help you, but I cannot."

Off I wandered through the streets of Cardigan, back to the dreary railway station. There was a two-hour wait for a train, but at last I arrived home to report, once again, no job. The next day I went back to the Employment Agency. The man sitting at his desk—did he ever move? I wondered, said, "I say, Old Boy, we simply cannot talk here. Take me out to lunch and I may be able to tell you something, what?"

For more than an hour I loitered about in the street outside, looking in the windows, and wishing that my feet would stop aching. A London policeman sourly watched me from the other side of the street, apparently unable to decide if I was a harmless individual or a prospective bank robber. Perhaps his feet were aching too! At last the Man was separated from his desk and came clattering down the creaky stairs. "A Number Seventy-Nine, Old Boy, we will take a Number Seventy-Nine. I know a nice little place, quite moderate for the service they give." We walked up the street, boarded a "79" bus, and soon reached our destination, one of those restaurants in a side street just off a main thoroughfare where the smaller the building the higher the charge. The Man Without his Desk and I had our lunch, mine a very frugal one and his exceedingly ample, then, with a sigh of satisfaction, he said, "You know, Old Boy, you fellows expect to get good appointments, but do you ever think that if the appointments available were that good, we of the staff would take them first? Our own jobs do not allow us to live in comfort, you know."

"Well," I said, "there must be some way of obtaining employment in this benighted city or outside it."

"Your trouble is that you look different, you attract attention. You also look ill. Maybe it would help if you shaved off your beard." He gazed at me reflectively, obviously wondering how to make a graceful exit. Suddenly he looked at his watch and jumped to his feet in alarm; "I say, Old Boy, I must simply fly, the old Slave Master will be watching y'know." He patted my arm and said, "Ta! Ta! Don't waste money coming to us, we simply have no jobs except for waiters and their ilk!" With that he turned in a whirl and was gone, leaving me to pay his quite considerable bill.

154

I wandered out and along the street. For want of something better to do, I looked at small advertisements in a shop window. "Young widow with small child wants work . . ." "Man, able to undertake intricate carvings, needs commissions." "Lady Masseuse gives treatment at home." (I'll bet she does, I thought!) As I walked away, I pondered the question; if the orthodox agencies, bureaux, exchanges etc., could not help me, then why not try an advertisement in a shop window. "Why not?" said my poor tired feet as they pounded hollowly on the hard, unsympathetic pavement.

That night, at home, I racked my brains trying to work out how to live and how to make enough money to carry on with Aura research. At last, I typed six postcards saying, "Doctor of Medicine (Not British Registered) offers help in psychological cases. Enquire within." I did another six which read, "Professional man, very widely traveled, scientific qualifications, offers services for anything unusual.

Excellent references. Write Box—" The next day, with the advertisements prominently displayed in certain strategic windows in London shops, I sat back to await results. They came. I managed to obtain enough psychological work to keep me going and the flickering fires of our finances slowly improved. As a sideline I did free-lance advertising, and one of the greatest pharmaceutical firms in England gave me part-time work. The very generous and human Director, a doctor, whom I saw, would have taken me on but for the Staff Insurance Scheme which was in force. I was too old and too sick. The strain of taking over a body was terrible. The strain of having the molecules of the "new" body exchanged for those of my own was almost more than I could stand, yet, in the interests of science, I stuck it out. More frequently now I traveled in the astral to Tibet by night or on week-ends when I knew that I should not be disturbed, for to disturb the body of one who is astral traveling can so easily be fatal. My solace was in the company of those High Lamas who could see me in the astral, and my reward was in their commendation of my actions. On one such visit I was mourning the passing of a very much beloved pet, a cat with intelligence to put many humans to shame. An old lama, with me in the astral, smiled in sympathy, and said, "My Brother, do you not remember the Story of the Mustard Seed?" The Mustard Seed, yes! How well I remembered it, one of the teachings of our Faith. . .

The poor young woman had lost her first-born child. Almost demented with grief she wandered through the streets of the city, pleading for something, someone, to bring her son back to life. Some people turned away from her in pity, some sneered and mocked her, calling her insane that she should believe her child could be restored to life. She would not be consoled, and none could find words with which to ease her pain. At last an old priest, noting her

155

utter despair, called her and said, "There is only one man in the whole world who can help you. He is the Perfect One, the Buddha who resides at the top of that mountain. Go and see him."

The young bereaved mother, her body aching with the weight of her sorrow, slowly walked up the hard mountain path until at last she turned a corner and saw the Buddha seated upon a rock. Prostrating herself, she cried "Oh! Buddha! Bring my son back to life." The Buddha rose and gently touched the poor woman, saying, "Go down into the city. Go from house to house and bring to me a mustard seed from a house in which no one has ever died." The young woman shouted with exultation as she rose to her feet and hastened down the mountain side. She hurried to the first house and said, "The Buddha bids me bring a mustard seed from a house which has never known death."

"In this house," she was told, "many have died." At the next house she was told, "It is impossible to tell how many have died here, for this is an old house."

She went from house to house, throughout that street, to the next street, and the one after. Scarcely pausing for rest or food, she went through the city from house to house and she could not find a single house which had not at some time been visited by death.

Slowly she retraced her steps up the mountain slopes. The Buddha was, as before, sitting in meditation. "Have you brought the mustard seed?" He asked.

"No, nor do I seek it any more," she said. "My grief blinded me so that I thought that only I suffered and sorrowed."

"Then why have you again come to me?" asked the Buddha.

"To ask you to teach me the truth," she answered.

And the Buddha told her: "In all the world of man, and all the world of Gods, this alone is the Law: All things are impermanent."

Yes, I knew all the Teachings, but the loss of one dearly loved was still a loss. The old lama smiled again and said, "A beautiful Little Person shall come to you to cheer your extraordinary difficult and hard life. Wait!"

Some time after, several months after, we took the Lady Ku'ei into our home.

156

She was a Siamese kitten of surpassing beauty and intelligence. Brought up by us as one would bring up a human, she has responded as a good human would. Certainly she has lightened our sorrows and eased the burden of human treachery.

Free-lance work without any legal standing was difficult indeed. Patients subscribed to the view that; the Devil was ill, the Devil a monk would be. The Devil was well, the Devil was he! The stories which defaulting patients told to explain their non-payment would fill many books, and cause the critics to work overtime. I continued my search for permanent work.

"Oh!" said a friend, "you can do free-lance writing, "ghost" writing. Have you thought of that? A friend of mine has written a number of books, I will give you an introduction to him." Off I went to one of the great London Museums to see the friend. Into an office I was shown, and for a moment I thought I was in the Museum storeroom!

I was afraid to move in case I knocked something over, so I just sat and became weary of sitting. At last "the Friend" came in. "Books?" he said. "Free-lance writing? I'll put you in touch with my agent. He may be able to fix you up." He scribbled industriously, and then handed me a paper with an address upon it. Almost before I knew what had happened, I was outside the office. "Well," I thought, "Will this be another wild-goose chase?"

I looked at the piece of paper in my hand. Regent Street? Now, which end of the street would it be? I got out of the train at Oxford Circus, and with my usual luck, found that I was at the wrong end! Regent Street was crowded, people seemed to be milling round the entrance of the big stores. A Boys' Brigade or Salvation Army Band, I did not know which, was proceeding noisily down Conduit Street. I walked on, past the Goldsmiths and Silversmiths Company, thinking how a little of their wares would enable me to get on with research. Where the street curved to enter Piccadilly Circus I crossed the road and looked for that wretched number. Travel Agency, Shoe Shop, but no Authors' Agent. Then I saw the number, sandwiched in between two shops. In I went to a little vestibule at the far end of which was an open lift. There was a bell push, so I used it. Nothing happened. I waited perhaps five minutes and then pressed the button again.

A clatter of feet, "You brought me up from the coal 'ole!" said a voice. "I was just 'avin' a cup of tea. Which floor d'ye want?"

"Mr. B—," I said, "I do not know which floor." "Aw, third floor," said the man. " 'E's in, I took 'im up. This is it," he said, sliding open the iron gate. "Turn right, in that door." With that he disappeared back to his cooling tea.

I pushed open the door indicated and walked up to a little counter. "Mr. B—?" I said. "I have an appointment with him." The dark haired girl went off in search of Mr. B— and I looked around me. At the other side of the counter girls were drinking tea. An elderly man was being given instruction about delivering some parcels. There was a table behind me with a few magazines upon it—like in a dentist's waiting room, I thought—and on the wall was an advertisement for some publishers. The office space seemed to be littered with parcels of books, and newly-opened typescripts were in a neat row against a far wall.

"Mr. B— will be with you in a moment," said a voice, and I turned to smile my thanks to the dark-haired girl. At that moment a side door opened, and Mr. B— came in. I looked at him with interest for he was the first Authors' Agent I had ever seen—or heard of! He had a beard, and I could visualize him as an old Chinese Mandarin. Although an Englishman, he had the dignity and courtesy of an elderly, educated Chinese of which there is no peer in the West.

Mr. B— came, greeted me and shook my hand, and let me through the side door to a very small room which reminded me of a prison cell without the bars. "And now what can I do for you?" he asked.

"I want a job," I said.

He asked me questions about myself, but I could see from his aura that he had no job to offer, that he was being courteous because of the man who had introduced me. I showed him my Chinese papers, and his aura flickered with interest. He picked them up, examined them most carefully, and said, "You should write a book. I think I can get one commissioned for you." This was a shock which almost bowled me over; me write a book? Me? About me? I looked at his aura carefully in order to see if he really meant it or if it was just a polite "brush-off". His aura said that it was meant but that he had a doubt as to my writing ability. As I took my leave his last words were, "You really should write a book."

"Aw, don't look so glum" said the liftman. "The sun is shining outside. Didn't he want your book?"

"That's just the trouble," I replied, as I got out of the lift, "He did!"

I walked along Regent Street thinking that everyone was mad. Me write a book? Crazy! All I wanted was a job providing enough money to keep us alive and a little over so that I could do auric research, and all the offers I had was to write a silly book about myself.

Some time before I had answered an advertisement for a Technical Writer for instruction books in connection with aircraft. By the evening mail I received a letter asking me to attend for an interview on the morrow. "Ah!" I thought, "I may get this job at Crawley after all!"

Early the next morning, as I was having breakfast before going to Crawley, a letter dropped in the box. It was from Mr. B——. "You should write a book," the letter said. "Think it over carefully and come and see me again."

"Pah!" I said to myself, "I should hate to write a book!" Off I went to Clapham Station to get a train for Crawley.

The train was the slowest ever, to my mind. It seemed to dawdle at every station and grind along the stretches between as if the engine or the driver was at the last gasp. Eventually I arrived at Crawley. The day was swelteringly hot now and I had just missed the bus. The next one would be too late. I plodded along through the streets, being misdirected by person after person, because the firm I was going to see was in a very obscure place. At long last, almost too tired to bother, I reached a long, unkempt lane. Walking along it I finally reached a tumble-down house which looked as if a regiment of soldiers had been billeted there.

"You wrote an exceptionally good letter," said the man who interviewed me. "We wanted to see what sort of man could write a letter like that!"

I gasped at the thought that he had brought me all this way out of idle curiosity. "But you advertised for a Technical Writer," I said, "and I am willing for any test."

"Ah! Yes," said the man, "but we have had much trouble since that advertisement was inserted, we are reorganizing and shall not take on anyone for six months at least. But we thought you would like to come and see our firm."

"I consider you should pay my fare," I retorted, "as you have brought me here on a fool's errand."

"Oh, we cannot do that," he said. "You offered to come for an interview; we merely accepted your offer."

159

I was so depressed that the long walk back to the station seemed even longer. The inevitable wait for a train, and the slow journey back to Clapham. The train wheels beneath me seemed to say: "You should write a book, you should write a book, you should write a book." In Paris, France, there is another Tibetan lama who came to the West for a special purpose. Unlike me, circumstances decreed that he should evade all publicity. He does his job and very few people know that he was once a lama in a Tibetan lamasery at the foot of the Potala. I had written to him asking his opinion and—to anticipate a little—it was to the effect that I would be unwise to write.

Clapham Station looked dirtier and dingier than ever, in my unhappy state of mind. I walked down the ramp to the street, and went home. My wife took one glance at my face and asked no questions. After a meal, although I did not feel like eating, she said: "I telephoned Mr. B— this morning. He says you should do a synopsis and take it for him to see." Synopsis! The mere thought sickened me. Then I read the mail which had arrived. Two letters saying that "the position had been filled. Thank you for applying," and the letter from my lama friend in France.

I sat down at the battered old typewriter which I had "inherited" from my predecessor, and started to write. Writing to me is unpleasant, arduous. There is no "inspiration", nor have I any gift, I merely work harder than most at a subject, and the more I dislike it, the harder and faster I work so that it is the sooner completed.

The day drew to a weary end, the shadows of dusk filled the streets and were dispelled as the street lamps came on to shed a garish glow over houses and people. My wife switched on the light and drew the curtain. I typed on. At last, with stiff and aching fingers, I stopped. Before me I had a pile of pages, thirty of them, all closely typed. "There!" I exclaimed. "If that does not suit him I will give up the whole thing, and I hope it does not suit him!"

The next afternoon I called on Mr. B— again. He looked once more at my papers, then took the synopsis and settled back to read. Every so often he nodded his head approvingly, and when he had finished, said, very cautiously, "I think we may be able to get it placed. Leave it with me. In the meantime write the first chapter."

I did not know whether to be pleased or sorry as I walked down Regent Street towards Piccadilly Circus. Finances had reached a dangerously low point, yet I just hated the thought of writing about myself.

Two days later I received a letter from Mr. B— asking me to call, telling me that he had good news for me. My heart sank at the thought, so I was going to have to write that book after all! Mr. B— beamed benevolently upon me. "I have a contract for you," he said, "but first I would like to take you to see the publisher." Together we went off to another part of London and entered a street which used to be a fashionable district, with high houses. Now the houses were used as offices, and people who should have been living in them lived in remote districts. We walked along the street and stopped at an undistinguished-looking house. "This is it," said Mr. B—. We entered a dark hallway and mounted a curving flight of stairs to the first floor. At last we were shown in to Mr. Publisher, who seemed a little cynical at first, only gradually warming up. The interview was of short duration and then we were back on the street.

"Come back to my office—dear me! Where are my spectacles?" said Mr. B—, feverishly going through his pockets in search of the missing glasses. He sighed with relief as he found them, continuing, "Come back to the office, I have the contract ready to sign."

At last here was something definite, a contract to write a book. I decided that I would do my part, and hoped that the publisher would do his. Certainly The Third Eye has enabled Mr. Publisher to put "a little jam on it!"

The book progressed, I did a chapter at a time and took it in to Mr. B—. On a number of occasions I visited Mr. and Mrs. B—at their charming home, and I would here like particularly to pay tribute to Mrs. B—. She welcomed me, and few English people did that. She encouraged me, and she was the first English woman to do so. At all times she made me welcome, so—thank you, Mrs. B—!

My health had been deteriorating rapidly in London's climate. I struggled to hold on while finishing the book, using all my training to put aside illness for a while. With the book finished, I had my first attack of coronary thrombosis and nearly died. At a very famous London hospital the medical staff were puzzled indeed by many things about me, but I did not enlighten them; perhaps this book will!

"You must leave London," said the specialist. "Your life is in danger here. Get away to a different climate."

"Leave London?" I thought. "But where shall we go? At home we had a discussion, discussing ways and means and places to live. Several days later I had to return to the hospital for a final check. "When are you going?" asked the specialist. "Your condition will not improve here."

161

"I just do not know," I replied. "There are so many things to consider."

"There is only one thing to consider," he said impatiently, "Stay here and you will die. Move and you may live a little longer. Do you not understand that your condition is serious?"

Once again I had a heavy problem to face.

Chapter Ten

"Lobsang! Lobsang!" I turned restlessly in my sleep. The pain in my chest was acute, the pain of that clot. Gasping, I returned to consciousness. Returned to hear again, "Lobsang!"

"My!" I thought, "I feel terrible!"

"Lobsang," the voice went on. "Listen to me, lie back and listen to me."

I lay back wearily. My heart was pumping and my chest was thobbing in sympathy. Gradually, within the darkness of my lonely room, a figure manifested itself. First a blue glow, turning to yellow, then the materialized form of a man of my own age. "I cannot astral travel tonight," I said, "or my heart will surely cease to beat and my tasks not yet ended."

"Brother! We well know your condition, so I have come to you. Listen, you need not talk."

I leaned back against the bed-head, my breath coming in sobbing gasps. It was painful to take a normal breath, yet I had to breathe in order to live.

"We have discussed your problem among us," said the materialized lama. "There is an island off the English coast, an island which was once part of the lost continent of Atlantis. Go there, go there as quickly as you can. Rest a while in that friendly land before journeying to the continent of North America. Go not to the western shores whose coastline is washed by the turbulent ocean. Go to the green city and then beyond."

Ireland? Yes! An ideal place. I had always got on well with Irish people. Green city? Then the answer came to me; Dublin, from a great height, looked green because of Phoenix Park and because of the River Liffey flowing from the mountains down to the sea.

The lama smiled approvingly. "You must recover some part of your health, for there will be a further attack upon it. We would have you live so that the Task may be advanced, so that the Science of the Aura may come nearer to fruition. I will go now, but when you are a little recovered, it is desired that you visit again the Land of the Golden Light."

The vision faded from my sight, and my room was the darker for it, and more lonely. My sorrows had been great, my sufferings beyond the ability of most to bear or to understand. I leaned back, gazing unseeingly through the window. What had they said on a recent astral visit to Lhasa? Oh, yes! "You find it difficult to obtain employment? Of course you do, my brother, for you are not part of the Western world, you live on borrowed time. The man whose living space you have taken would have died in any case. Your need, temporarily for his body, more permanently for his living space, meant that he could leave the Earth with honour and with gain. This is not Kharma, my brother, but a task which you are doing upon this, your last life on Earth." A very hard life, too, I told myself.

In the morning I was able to cause some consternation or surprise by announcing, "We are going to live in Ireland. Dublin first, then outside Dublin."

I was not much help in getting things ready, I was very sick, and almost afraid to move for fear of provoking a heart attack. Cases were packed, tickets obtained, and at last we set off. It was good to be in the air again, and I found that breathing was much easier. The airline, with a "heart-case" passenger aboard, took no risks. There was an oxygen cylinder on the rack above my head.

The plane flew lower, and circled over a land of vivid green, fringed by milk-white surf. Lower still, and there was the rumble of an undercarriage being lowered, followed shortly by the screech of the tires touching the landing strip.

My thoughts turned to the occasion of my first entry to England, and my treatment by the Customs official. "What will this be like?" I mused. We taxied up to the airport buildings, and I was more than a little mortified to find a wheel-chair awaiting me. In Customs the officials looked hard at us and said, "How long are you staying?"

"We have come to live here," I replied.

There was no trouble, they did not even examine our belongings. The Lady Ku'ei fascinated them all as, serene and self possessed, she stood guard on our luggage. These Siamese cats, when properly trained and treated as beings, not just animals, are possessed of superlative intelligence. Certainly I prefer the Lady Ku'ei's friendship and loyalty to that of humans; she sits by me at night and awakens my wife if I am ill!

Our luggage was loaded on a taxi, and we were driven off to Dublin city. The

164

atmosphere of friendliness was very marked; nothing seemed to be too much trouble. I lay upon my bed in a room overlooking the grounds of Trinity College. On the road below my window, traffic moved at a sedate pace.

It took me some time to recover from the journey, but when I could get about, the friendly officials of Trinity College gave me a pass which enabled me to use their grounds and their magnificent library. Dublin was a city of surprises; one could buy almost anything there. There was a far greater variety of goods than there is in Windsor, Canada, or Detroit, U.S.A. After a few months, while I was writing Doctor from Lhasa, we decided to move to a very beautiful fishing village some twelve miles away. We were fortunate in obtaining a house overlooking Balscadden Bay, a house with a truly amazing view.

I had to rest a very great deal, and found it impossible to see through the windows with binoculars because of the distorting effect of the glass. A local builder, Brud Campbell, with whom I became very friendly, suggested plate glass. With that installed, I could rest on my bed and watch the fishing boats out in the bay. The whole expanse of harbor was within my view, with the Yacht Club, the harbor master's office and the lighthouse as prominent features. On a clear day I could see the Mountains of Mourne, away in British occupied Ireland, while, from Howth Head, I could dimly see the mountains of Wales far across the Irish Sea.

We bought a second-hand car and often journeyed up into the Dublin Mountain, enjoying the pure air and the beautiful scenery. On one such trip we heard of an elderly Siamese cat who was dying from an immense internal tumor. After much pressure, we managed to take her into our household. The best veterinary surgeon in the whole of Ireland examined her but thought she had only hours to live. I persuaded him to operate to remove the tumor caused by neglect and too many kittens. She recovered, and proved to have the sweetest nature of any person or animal I have ever met. Now, as I write, she is walking round like the gentle old lady she is. Quite blind, her beautiful blue eyes radiate intelligence and goodness. The Lady Ku'ei walks with her, or directs her telepathically so that she does not bump into things or hurt herself. We call her Granny Greywhiskers as she is so much like an elderly granny walking around, enjoying the evening of her life, after raising many families.

Howth brought me happiness, happiness that I had not known before. Mr. Loftus, the policeman, or "Guard" as they are called in Ireland, frequently stopped to chat. He was always a welcome visitor. A big man, as smart as a Guard at Buckingham Palace, he had a reputation for utter fairness and utter

165

fearlessness. He would come in, when off duty, and talk of far-off places. His "My God, Doctor, ye've brains to throw away!" was a delight to hear. I had been badly treated by the police of many countries, and Guard Loftus, of Howth, Ireland, showed me that there were good policemen as well as the bad which I had known.

My heart was showing signs of distress again, and my wife wanted the telephone installed. Unfortunately all the lines of "The Hill" were in use so we could not have one. One afternoon there came a knock at the door, and a neighbour, Mrs. O'Grady, said, "I hear you want the telephone and cannot get it. Use ours at any time you like—here is a key to the house!" The Irish treated us well. Mr. and Mrs. O'Grady were always trying to do something for us, trying to make our stay in Ireland even more pleasant. It has been our pleasure and our privilege to bring Mrs. O'Grady to our home in Canada for an all too brief visit.

Suddenly, shockingly, I was taken violently ill. The years in prison camps, the immense strains I had undergone, and the unusual experiences had combined to make my heart condition serious indeed. My wife rushed up to the O'Grady's house and telephoned a doctor to come quickly. In a surprisingly short time, Dr. Chapman came into my bedroom, and with the efficiency that comes only from long years of practice, got busy with his hypodermic! Dr. Chapman was one of the "old school" of doctors, the "family doctor" who had more knowledge in his little finger than half a dozen of the "factory produced" State aided specimens so popular today. With Dr. Chapman and me it was a case of "friends at first sight!" slowly, under his care, I recovered enough to get out of bed. Then came a round of visiting specialists in Dublin. Someone in England had told me never to trust myself to an Irish doctor. I did trust myself, and had better medical treatment than in any other country of the world. The personal, the human touch was there, and that is better than all the mechanical coldness of the young doctors.

Brud Campbell had erected a good stone wall round our grounds, replacing a broken one, because we were sorely troubled by trippers from England. People used to come on excursions from Liverpool and enter the gardens of the Howth people and camp there! We had one "tripper" who caused some amusement. One morning there was a loud knock at the door. My wife answered it, and found a German woman outside. She tried to push her way in, but failed. Then she announced that she was going to camp on our doorstep until she was allowed in to "sit at the feet of Lobsang Rampa." As I was in bed, and certainly did not want anyone sitting at my feet, she was asked to go. By afternoon she was still there. Mr. Loftus came along, looking very fierce and efficient, and persuaded the woman to go down the hill, get on a bus for Dublin, and not come back!

They were busy days, with me trying not to overtax my strength. Doctor from Lhasa was now completed, but letters were coming in from all over the world. Pat the Postman would come wheezing to the door, after the long climb up the hill. "Ah! Good marnin' to ye," he would say to whoever answered his knock, "And how is Himself today? Ah, sure the letters are breakin' me back!"

One night as I lay upon my bed watching the twinkling lights of Portmarnock, and of the ships far out to sea, I was suddenly aware of an old man sitting gazing at me. He smiled as I turned in his direction. "I have come," he said, "to see how you progress, for it is desired that you go again to the Land of the Golden Light. How do you feel?"

"I think I can manage, with a little effort," I replied.

"Are you coming with me?"

"No," he answered, "for your body is more valuable than ever before, and I am to stay here and guard it."

During the past few months I had suffered greatly. One of the causes of my suffering was a matter which would cause a Westerner to recoil in disbelief; the whole changeover of my original body had taken place. The substitute body had been teleported elsewhere and allowed to fall to dust. For those who are sincerely interested, it is an old Eastern art and can be read about in certain books.

I lay for a few moments, collecting my strength. Outside the window a late fishing boat went phut-phutting by. The stars were bright, and Ireland's Eye was bathed in moonlight. The old man smiled and said, "A pleasant view you have here!" I nodded silently, straightened my spine, folded my legs beneath me, and drifted off like a puff of smoke. For a time I hovered above the headland, gazing down at the moonlit countryside. Ireland's Eye, the island just off the coast, farther out the Island of Lambay. Behind glowed the bright lights of Dublin, a modern, well-lit city indeed. As I rose higher, slowly, I could see the magnificent curve of Killenye Bay, so reminiscent of Naples, and beyond— Greystones and Wicklow. Off I drifted, out of this world, out of this space and time. On, to a plane of existence which cannot be described in the languages of this three-dimensional world.

It was like going from darkness into the sunlight. My Guide, the Lama Mingyar Dondup, was awaiting me. "You have done so well, Lobsang, and have suffered so much," he said. "In a short time you will be returning here not to leave again. The struggle has been worthwhile." We moved together through the glorious countryside, moved to the Hall of Memories where there was much yet to learn.

For some time we sat and talked, my Guide, an august group, and I. "Soon," said one, "you will go to the Land of the Red Indians and there we have another task for you. For a few short hours refresh yourself here, for your ordeals of late have sorely taxed your strength."

"Yes," remarked another, "and be not upset by those who would criticize you, for they know not whereof they speak, being blinded by the self imposed ignorance of the West. When Death shall close their eyes, and they become born to the Greater Life, then indeed will they regret the sorrows and troubles they have so needlessly caused."

As I returned to Ireland the land was yet in darkness, with just a few faint streaks shooting across the morning sky. Along the long stretch of sands at Clontarf the surf was breaking with a sighing moan. The Head of Howth loomed up, a darker shape in the pre-dawn darkness. As I floated down, I glanced at our rooftop. "Dear me!" I remarked to myself. "The seagulls have bent my aerial rods. I shall have to call in Brud Campbell to put them straight." The old man was still sitting by my bedside. Mrs. Fifi Greywhiskers was sitting on the end of my bed as if on guard. As I entered my body and re-animated it, she came up to me, rubbed against me and purred. She uttered a low call, and Lady Ku'ei came in, jumped on the bed and took up her station on my lap. The old man gazed down upon them in marked affection and remarked, "Truly entities of a high order. I must go, my brother."

The morning post brought a savage assessment from the Irish Income Tax Office. The only Irish people I dislike are those connected with the Tax Office; they seemed to me to be so unhelpful, so unnecessarily officious. For writers in Ireland, the tax is absolutely penal, and it is a tragedy, because Ireland could well do with those who would spend money. Tax or no tax, I would rather live in Ireland than in any other place in the world except Tibet.

"We will go to Canada," I said. Gloomy looks greeted that statement. "How will we take the cats?" I was asked.

"By air, of course, they will travel with us," I answered.

The formalities were considerable, the delays long. The Irish officials were helpful in the extreme, the Canadians not at all helpful. The American Consulate offered far more help than did the Canadian. We were fingerprinted and investigated, then we went for our medical examinations. I failed. "Too many scars," said the doctor. "You will have to be X-rayed." The Irish doctor who X-rayed me looked at me with compassion. "You must have had a terrible life." he said. "Those scars . . .! I shall have to report my findings to the Canadian Board of Health. In view of your age I anticipate that they will admit you to Canada, subject to certain conditions."

The Lady Ku'ei and Mrs. Fifi Greywhiskers were examined by a veterinary surgeon and both pronounced fit. While waiting for a ruling about my case, we made enquiries about taking the cats on the plane with us. Only Swissair would agree, so we provisionally booked with them.

Days later I was called to the Canadian Embassy. A man looked at me sourly. "You are sick!" he said. "I have to be sure that you will not be a charge on the country." He fiddled and fiddled, and then, as if with immense effort, said, "Montreal has authorized your entry provided you report to the Board of Health immediately you arrive, and take whatever treatment they say you need. If you don't agree, you can't go," he said, hopefully. It seemed very strange to me that so many Embassy officials in other countries are so needlessly offensive; after all, they are merely hired servants, one cannot always call them "civil servants!"

We kept our intentions private; only our closest friends knew that we were going and knew where we were going. As we knew to our cost, it was almost a case that if we sneezed, a press reporter would come hammering at the door to ask why. For the last time we drove around Dublin, and around the beauty spots of Howth. It was indeed a wrench to even think of leaving, but none of us are here for pleasure. A very efficient firm in Dublin had agreed to drive us to Shannon in a bus, us, the cats, and our luggage.

A few days before Christmas we were ready to go. Our old friend Mr. Loftus came to say good-bye, and to see us off. If there were not tears in his eyes, then I was much mistaken. Certainly I felt that I was parting from a very dear friend. Mr. and Mrs. O'Grady came to see us, Mr. O'Grady taking the day off for that purpose. "Ve O'G" was openly upset, Paddy was trying to hide his emotion with a show of joviality which deceived no one. I locked the door, gave the key to Mr. O'Grady to mail to the solicitor, got in the bus and we drove away from the happiest time of my life since I left Tibet, drove away from the nicest group of people I had met in long, long years.

The bus rushed along the smooth highway to Dublin, threading through the city's courteous traffic. On, and into open country skirting the mountains.

169

For hours we drove on, the friendly driver, efficient at his task, pointing out landmarks and being solicitous of our welfare and comfort. We stopped half way for tea. The Lady Ku'ei likes to sit up high and watch the traffic and yell encouragement to whoever is driving her. Mrs. Fifi Greywhiskers prefers to sit quietly and think. With the bus stopped for tea, there was great consternation. Why had we stopped? Was everything all right?

We continued on, for the road was long and Shannon far distant. Darkness came upon us and slowed us somewhat. Late in the evening we arrived at Shannon Airport, left our main luggage, and were driven to the accommodation we had booked for the night and the next day. Because of my health and the two cats we stayed at Shannon a night and a day, leaving on the next night. We had a room each, fortunately they had communicating doors, because the cats did not know where they wanted to be. For a time they wandered around, sniffing like vacuum cleaners, "reading" all about people who had previously used the rooms, then they fell silent and were soon asleep.

I rested the next day, and looked round the Airport. The "Duty-Free" Shop interested me, but I could not see the use of it; if one bought an article one had to declare it somewhere and then pay duty, so what was the gain?

The Swissair officials were helpful and efficient, the formalities were soon completed and all we waited for was the plane. Midnight came and went, one o'clock. At one-thirty we were taken aboard a big Swissair plane, we, and our two cats. People were most impressed by them, by their self-control and composure. Not even the noise of the engines disturbed them. Soon we were speeding along the runway faster and faster. The land dropped away, the River Shannon flowed briefly beneath a wing and was gone. Before us the wide Atlantic surged, leaving a white surf along the coast of Ireland. The engine note changed, long flames trailed from the glowing exhaust pipes. The nose tilted slightly. The two cats looked silently at me; was there anything to worry about, they wondered. This was my seventh Atlantic crossing, and I smiled reassuringly at them. Soon they curled up and went to sleep.

The long night wore on. We were traveling with the darkness, for us the night would be some twelve hours of darkness. The cabin lights dimmed, leaving us with the blue glow and a faint prospect of sleep. The droning engines carried us on, on at thirty-five thousand feet above the gray, restless sea. Slowly the pattern of stars changed. Slowly a faint lightening was observed in the distant sky on the edge of the Earth's curve. Bustling movement in the galley, the clatter of dishes, then, slowly, like a plant growing, came the lights. The amiable Purser came walking through, ever attentive to his passengers' comfort. The efficient cabin crew came round with breakfast. There is no nation like the Swiss for efficiency in the air, for attending to the passengers' wants, and for providing truly excellent food. The cats sat up and were all attention at the thought of eating again.

Far off to the right a hazy gray line appeared and rapidly grew larger. New York! Inevitably I thought of the first time I had come to America, working my way as a ship's engineer. Then the skyscrapers of Manhattan had towered heavenwards, impressing with their size. Now, where were they? Not those little dots, surely? The great plane circled, and a wing dipped. The engines changed their pitch. Gradually we sank lower and lower. Gradually buildings on the ground took shape, what had appeared to be a desolate waste resolved itself into Idlewild International Airport. The skilled Swiss Pilot set the plane down with just a faint scrunch of tyres. Gently we taxied along the runway to the Airport buildings. "Keep your seats, please!" said the Purser. A gentle "thud" as the mobile stairway came to rest against the fuselage, a metallic scraping, and the cabin door was swung open. "Good-bye," said the cabin crew, lining the exit, "Travel with us again!" Slowly we filed down the stairway and into the Administrative Buildings.

Idlewild was like a railway station gone mad. People rushed everywhere, jostling any that stood in their path. An attendant stepped forward, "This way, Customs clearance first." We were lined up by the side of moving platforms. Great masses of luggage suddenly appeared, moving along the platforms, stretching from the entrance to the Customs man. The Officials walked along, rummaging through open cases. "Where you from, folks?" said an Officer to me.

"Dublin, Ireland," I replied.

"Where you going?"

"Windsor, Canada," I said.

"Okay, got any pornographic pictures?" he asked suddenly.

With him settled, we had to show Passports and Visas. It reminded me of a Chicago meat packing factory, the way people were "processed."

Before we left Ireland we had booked seats on an American plane to fly us to Detroit. They agreed to take the cats in the plane with us. Now the officials of the Airline concerned repudiated our tickets, and refused to take our two cats who had crossed the Atlantic without trouble or fuss. For a time it seemed that we were stuck in New York, the Airline was not remotely interested. I saw an advertisement for "Air taxis to anywhere" from La Guardia Airfield.

Taking an airport limousine we went the several miles to a Motel just outside La Guardia. "Can we bring in our cats?" we asked the man at the registration desk. He looked at them, two demure little ladies, and said, "Sure, sure, they're welcome!" The Lady Ku'ei and Mrs. Fifi Greywhiskers were glad indeed to have a chance to walk about and investigate two more rooms.

The strain of the journey was now telling upon me. I retired to bed. My wife crossed the road to La Guardia, trying to find what an air taxi would cost, and when we could be taken. Eventually she returned looking worried. "It is going to cost a lot of money!" she said.

"Well, we cannot stay here, we have to move," I replied.

She picked up the telephone and soon arranged that on the morrow we would fly by air taxi to Canada.

We slept well that night. The cats were quite unconcerned, it even seemed that they were enjoying themselves. In the morning, after breakfast, we were driven across the road to the Airport. La Guardia is immense, with a plane taking off or landing every minute of the day. At last we found the place from whence we were to go, and we, our cats, and our luggage were loaded aboard a small twin- engined plane. The pilot, a little man with a completely shaven head, nodded curtly to us, and off we taxied to a runway. For some two miles we taxied and then pulled in to a bay to wait our turn to take off. The pilot of a big inter-continental plane waved to us, and spoke hurriedly into his microphone. Our pilot uttered some words which I cannot repeat, and said, "We have a —— puncture."

The air was rent by a screaming police siren. A police cruiser raced madly along a service road and pulled up alongside us with a mad squeal of tires. "Police? What have we done now?" I asked myself. More sirens, and the fire brigade arrived, men spilling off as the machines slowed. The policemen came across and spoke to our pilot. They moved away to the fire engine, and at last the police and firemen moved off. A repair car raced along, jacked up the plane in which we were sitting, removed the offending wheel-and raced off. For two hours we sat there waiting for the wheel to be returned to us. At last the wheel was on, the pilot started his engines again, and we took off. Off we flew, over the Alleghany range, headed first for Pittsburg. Right over the mountains the fuel gauge—right in front of me—dropped to zero and started knocking against the stop. The pilot seemed blandly unaware of it. I pointed it out and he said, in a whisper, "Ah, sure, we can always go down!" Minutes after we came to a level space in the mountains, a space where many light planes were parked. The pilot circled once, and landed, taxiing along to the petrol pumps. We stopped just long enough to have the plane refuelled, and then off again from the snow-covered, frozen runway. Deep banks of snow lined the sides, great drifts were in the valleys. A short flight, and we were over Pittsburg. We were sick of traveling, stiff and weary. Only the Lady Ku'ei was alert, she sat and looked out of a window and appeared pleased with everything.

With Cleveland beneath us, we saw Lake Erie right in front. Great masses of ice were piled up, while fantastic cracks and fissures ran across the frozen lake. The pilot, taking no risks, made course for Pelee Island, half way across the lake. From there he flew on to Amherstburg, and on to Windsor Airport. The Airport looked strangely quiet. There was no bustle of activity. We moved up to the Customs Building, alighted from the plane, and went inside. A solitary Customs man was just going off duty—it was after six at night. Gloomily he contemplated our baggage. "There is no Immigration Officer here," he said. "You will have to wait until one comes." We sat and waited. The slow minutes crawled by. Half an hour, time itself seemed to stand still, we had had no food or drink since eight o'clock that morning. The clock struck seven. A relief Customs man came in and dawdled about. "I can't do a thing until the Immigration Officer has cleared you," he said. Time seemed to be going more slowly. Seven-thirty. A tall man came in and went to the Immigration Offlcer's office. Looking frustrated and a little red in the face, he came out to the Customs man. "I can't get the desk open," he said. For a time they muttered together, trying keys, banging pushing. At last, in desperation, they took a screwdriver and forced the desk lock. It was the wrong desk, it was quite empty.

Eventually the forms were found. Wearily we filled them in, signing here, signing there. The Immigration Officer stamped our Passports "Landed Immigrant".

"Now you go to the Customs Officer," he said. Cases to open, boxes to unlock. Forms to show, giving details of our belongings as "Settlers"—More rubber stamps, and at last we were free to enter Canada at Windsor, Ontario. The Customs Officer warmed up considerably when he knew we came from Ireland. Of Irish descent himself, with his Irish parents still living, he asked many questions and— wonder of wonders—he helped carry our luggage to the waiting car.

Outside the Airport it was bitter, the snow was thick upon the ground. Just across the Detroit River the skyscrapers towered aloft, a mass of light as all the offices and rooms were illuminated, for Christmas was at hand.

We drove down the wide Ouellette Avenue, the main street of Windsor. The River was invisible, and it looked as if we were going to drive straight to America. The fellow who was driving us did not seem at all sure of his directions; missing a main intersection, he made a remarkable maneuver which made our hair stand on end. Eventually we reached our rented house and were glad indeed to alight.

Very soon I had a communication from the Board of Health demanding my presence, threatening terrible things —including deportation—if I did not attend. Unfortunately threats seem to be the main hobby of the Ontario officials, that is why we are now going to move again, to a more friendly Province.

At the Board of Health I was X-rayed, more details were taken, and at last I was allowed to go home again. Windsor has a terrible climate, and that and the attitude of officials soon decided us to move as soon as this book is written.

Now the Rampa Story is finished. The truth has been told, as in my other two books. I have much that I could tell the Western world, for in astral traveling I have touched merely upon the fringe of things which are possible. Why send out spy planes with its attendant risks when one can travel in the astral and see inside a council chamber? One can see and one can remember. Under certain circumstances one can teleport articles, if it be wholly for good. But Western man scoffs at things he does not understand, yells "faker" to those who have abilities which he himself does not possess, and works himself into a frenzy of vituperation against those who dare to be in any way "different".

Happily I put aside my typewriter and settled down to entertain the Lady Ku'ei and blind Mrs. Fifi Greywhiskers who both had waited so patiently.

That night, telepathically, came the Message again. "Lobsang! You have not yet finished your book!" My heart sank, I hated writing, knowing that so few people had the capacity to perceive Truth. I write of the things which the human mind can accomplish. Even the elementary stages described in this book will be disbelieved, yet if one were to be told that the Russians had sent a man to Mars, that would be believed! Man is afraid of the powers of Man's mind, and can contemplate only the worthless things like rockets and space satellites. Better results can be achieved through mental processes.

174

"Lobsang! Truth? Do you remember the Hebrew tale? Write it down, Lobsang, and write also of what could be, in Tibet!"

A Rabbi, famed for his learning and his wit, was once asked why he so often illustrated a great truth by telling a simple story. "That," said the wise Rabbi, "can best be illustrated by a parable! A parable about Parable. There was a time when Truth went among people unadorned, as naked as Truth. Whoever saw Truth turned away in fear or in shame because they could not face him. Truth wandered among the peoples of the Earth, unwelcome, rebuffed, and unwanted. One day, friendless and alone, he met Parable strolling happily along, dressed in fine and many colored clothes. 'Truth, why are you so sad, so miserable?' asked Parable, with a cheerful smile. 'Because I am so old and so ugly that people avoid me,' said Truth, dourly. 'Nonsense!' laughed Parable. 'That is not why people avoid you. Borrow some of my clothes, go among people and see what happens.' So Truth donned some of Parable's lovely garments, and wherever he now went he was welcome." The wise old Rabbi smiled and said, "Men cannot face naked Truth, they much prefer him disguised in the clothing of Parable."

"Yes, yes, Lobsang, that is a good translation of our thoughts, now the Tale."

The cats wandered off to sit on their beds and wait until I really had finished. I picked up the typewriter again, inserted the paper, and continued . . .

From afar the Watcher sped, gleaming a ghostly blue as he flashed over continents and oceans, leaving the sunlit side of the Earth for the dark. In his astral state he could be seen only to those who were clairvoyant, yet he could see all and, returning later to his body, remember all. He dropped, immune to cold, untroubled by thinness of air, to the shelter of a high peak, and waited.

The first rays of the morning sun glinted briefly on the highest pinnacles of rock, turning them to gold, reflecting a myriad of colors from the snow in the crevices. Vague streaks of light shot across the lightening sky as slowly the sun peeped across the distant horizon.

Down in the valley strange things were happening. Carefully shielded lights moved about, as if on trailers. The silver thread of the Happy River gleamed faintly, throwing back flecks of light. There was much activity, strange, concealed activity. The lawful inhabitants of Lhasa hid in their homes, or lay under guard in the forced-labor barracks.

Gradually the sun moved upon its path. Soon the first rays, probing downwards, glinted upon a strange shape that loomed up far across the

Valley floor. As the sunlight grew brighter the Watcher saw the immense shape more clearly. It was huge, cylindrical, and on its pointed end, facing the heavens above, were painted eyes and a tooth- ensnagged mouth. For centuries the Chinese seamen had painted eyes upon their ships. Now, upon this Monster the eyes glared hate.

The sun moved on. Soon the whole Valley was bathed in light. Strange metal structures were being towed away from the Monster, now only partly enshrouded in its cradle. The immense rocket, towering on its fins, looked sinister, deadly. At its base technicians with headphones on were running about like a colony of disturbed ants. A siren sounded shrilly, and the echoes rebounded, from rock to rock, from mountain wall to mountain wall, blending into a fearful, horrendous cacophony of sound which built up, becoming louder and louder. Soldiers, guards, laborers, turned on the instant and ran as fast as they could to the shelter of the distant rocks.

Halfway up the mountain side the light glinted on a little group of men clustered around radio equipment. A man picked up a microphone and spoke to the inhabitants of a great concrete and steel shelter lying half concealed about a mile from the rocket. A droning voice counted out the seconds and then stopped.

For scant moments nothing happened, there was peace. The lazy tendrils of vapor seeping from the rocket were the only things that moved. A gush of steam, and a roaring that grew louder and louder, starting small rock-falls. The earth itself seemed to vibrate and groan. The sound became louder and louder until it seemed that the ear-drums must shatter under such intensity. A great gout of flame and steam appeared from the base of the rocket, obscuring all below. Slowly, as if with immense, with stupendous effort, the rocket rose. At one time it seemed to be standing stationary on its tail of fire, then it gathered speed and climbed up into the quaking heavens, booming and roaring defiance to mankind. Up, up it went, leaving a long train of steam and smoke. The scream vibrated among the mountain tops long after all sight of it had gone.

The group of technicians on the mountainside feverishly watched their radarscopes, yammered into their microphones, or scanned the skies with high-power binoculars. Far, far overhead a vagrant gleam of light flashed down as the mighty rocket turned and settled on its course.

Scared faces appeared from behind rocks. Little groups of people congregated, with all distinction between guards and slave-laborers temporarily forgotten. The minutes ticked on. Technicians switched off their

176

radar sets, for the rocket had soared far beyond their range. The minutes ticked on.

Suddenly the technicians leapt to their feet, gesticulating madly, forgetting to switch on the microphones in their excitement. The rocket, with an atomic warhead, had landed in a far distant, peace-loving country. The land was a shambles, with cities wrecked, and people vaporized to incandescent gas. The Chinese Communists, with the loudspeakers full on, screamed and shouted with glee, forgetting all reserve in the joy of their dreadful accomplishment. The first stage of war had ended, the second was about to start. Exulting technicians rushed to make the second rocket ready.

Is it fantasy? It could be fact! The higher the launching point of a rocket; the less the atmosphere impedes it and so it takes far, far less fuel. A rocket launched from the flat lands of Tibet, seventeen thousand feet above sea level, would be more efficient than one launched from the lowlands. So the Communists have an incalculable advantage over the rest of the world, they have the highest and most efficient sites from which to launch rockets either into space or at other countries.

China has attacked Tibet—not conquered it—so that she shall have this great advantage over Western powers. China has attacked Tibet so that she shall have access to India, when she is ready, and perhaps drive on through India to Europe. It could be that China and Russia will combine to make a pincer thrust which could crush out the free life of all countries that stood in their way. It could be—unless something is done soon. Poland? Pearl Harbor? Tibet? "Experts" would have said that such enormities could not be. They were wrong! Are they going to be wrong again?